CAT FIRST AID

A GUIDE TO EMERGENCY
TREATMENT & GENERAL HEALTH CARE

**GEORGE E. BOYLE, V.M.D.,
WITH CHARLES L. BLOOD**

A Storey Publishing Book

STOREY

Storey Communications, Inc.
Pownal, Vermont 05261

Cover design by Leslie Morris Noyes
Text design by Wanda Harper
Production by Carol Jessop
Illustrations by Carol Jessop

Printed in the United States by R.R. Donnelley

First Printing, October 1990

Library of Congress Cataloging-in-Publication Data

Boyle, George E.
    Cat first aid: A guide to emergency treatment & general health care/ George E. Boyle, with Charles L. Blood.
      p.   cm.
    "A Storey Publishing Book".
    Includes index.
    ISBN 0-88266-626-6 (pbk.)
    1. Cats—Wounds and injuries—Treatment. 2. Cats—Diseases—Treatment. 3. Cats—Health. 4. First aid for animals. 5. Veterinary emergencies. I. Blood, Charles L. II. Title.
SF958.B69
636.8'0896—dc20   90-50019
                                                CIP

CONTENTS

1. **CATVEATE EMPTOR AND OTHER FORMS OF PREVENTIVE MEDICINE** 1

   Acquiring a Cat 3
   Congenital Disorders 4
   Acquiring a Purebred Cat 9
   Traveling with Your Cat 11
   Diet 14

2. **TRAUMATIC ACCIDENTS** 17

   Moving an Injured Cat 20
   Restraining an Injured Cat 21
   Cats and Cars 25
   Specific Injuries 27
   Other Cat-tastrophes 45

3. **PREVENTABLE CAT-TASTROPHES** 71

   General Skin Problems 73
   Claws and Nails 82
   Oral Problems 84
   Vomiting and Diarrhea 89
   Internal Parasites 90
   Feline Asthma 94
   The Cardiovascular System 94
   The Urinary System 96
   The Reproductive System 99
   Neurological Problems 103
   An Overview of Poisons 107

   DRUG DOSAGES 116

   INDEX 119

1

CATVEATE
EMPTOR
AND OTHER FORMS OF
PREVENTIVE
MEDICINE

If happiness for some people is a warm puppy, total bliss for other people is a fluffy kitten. Yet, nobody really *owns* a cat

Venerated in ancient Egyptian and Norse religions, the cat is a relative newcomer to domesticity: about 5,000 years compared to 50,000 for dogs. The cat is the most exclusive meat eater among all the carnivores and the most highly adept at hunting and devouring its prey.

Unlike dogs, who crave and even survive on their owner's affection, a cat chooses to tolerate your presence, when and if it's convenient. A cat may accept your food and shelter, but it will never let you forget it doesn't really need you to survive. A cat's attitude about life and the people it's living with is very simple: "I come first."

In defense of the domestic feline, we are speaking about the nature of the beast in general. Not of the cat who already shares your life, nor of the cat you may acquire. That, of course, would be a different breed of cat.

If you are already a cat person, what follows should be remembered when the time comes to replace your present cat. If you're thinking of becoming a cat person, consider the recommendations to prospective cat owners below carefully and then make your decision.

ACQUIRING A CAT

Of course, there is always the friend with a litter of absolutely adorable kittens — one of which is exactly right for you — or the irresistible stray that hits you up for a free meal and decides you're worthy of its continued presence. But let's suppose neither of the above occurs and you're shopping around. Whether you're after a mixed breed or a purebred is based on your reason or reasons for having a cat. Assuming for the moment you have no need or wish to own a purebred, you will probably be shopping in a pet shop or animal shelter. Not that a purebred can't be found in an animal shelter or a pet shop. They most certainly can, but we'll speak at some length of purebreds later. Right now, our subject is that sturdy, selectively independent, highly resilient occupant of unknown millions of households: the American domestic shorthair. Striped, spotted, or solid in color.

Shelters and many pet shops receive a large number of stray animals and lots of kittens from unwanted litters. These animals are usually received with little or no knowledge of health background. Therefore, they are more apt to have infections or congenital problems. If you purchase such an animal, you are protected by law. You have two weeks from date of purchase to have a veterinarian examine the cat or kitten. If it is found unfit, you can return it for refund or exchange. Note that the law is often circumvented by a seller who will identify what you have paid as an "adoption fee." If you have any doubts regarding the animal's health, avoid the term "adoption" and secure a bill of sale as proof of purchase. This will give you greater leverage if the animal doesn't check out.

Actually, any cat, adult or otherwise, with or without a medical history, should be taken to a veterinarian for a complete checkup twenty-four to forty-eight hours after you've acquired it. If medical records exist, bring them. At the very least, bring a stool sample.

CONGENITAL DISORDERS

These can be defined as abnormalities occuring during pregnancy that are obvious at birth or soon afterwards. Not all such defects are hereditary. Many are due to outside influences on the fetus, including chemicals or drugs that might be given to or accidentally ingested by the mother-to-be, or the lack of proper vaccinations. Another recognized cause of birth defects are viral infections — feline leukemia and distemper in particular — which cause central nervous system disorders or circulatory system problems. Due to the extreme susceptibility of the unborn, veterinarians don't like to vaccinate pregnant cats. If there's no choice, the vaccination may be given after the cat's owner has been made aware of the risks, but this most basic of preventive measures should be taken long before the possibility of pregnancy exists.

SPECIFIC BIRTH DEFECTS

Polydactylism. In simple language, too many toes. Usually harmless unless they are manifested as extra "thumbs," the toes higher up on the paw. These can easily become ingrown and will then need care to prevent infection (see "Claws and Nails," page 82). The opposite of polydactylism is too few toes: In the extreme, this defect can result in a thalidomide-type kitten lacking fully developed limbs.

Patent Fontanal. A soft spot in the top of the kitten's skull. It may eventually close up. More often than not they do but, until they do, great care is required in handling. The condition can be detected by very gently pressing a finger over the top of the skull.

Hydroencephalus. The skull itself is enlarged due to an improper drainage system within the brain. This condition is usually fatal at birth. If it isn't, a kitten so afflicted should not be forced to suffer the consequences of trying to live with it.

Cleft Palate. A very common disorder, this occurs in varying degrees by failure of the roof of the mouth to close from side to side. If the gap is narrow, it can be repaired surgically, and the animal can look forward to a normal life. Signs of a cleft palate are discernible early, so watch out for them: The kitten will be unable to suckle and the mother's milk will run out of its nose.

Hernias. These result from the failure of one of the internal body openings to close fully. The most common is the *umbilical hernia.* If small, it's evidenced by a "bulging belly button." If large, the intestine can get caught up in the hernia and become strangulated. The condition can be surgically corrected in young kittens. Another kind of hernia, the *diaphragmatic hernia*, prevents the diaphragm from separating the abdominal organs from those of the chest. Not easily detectable, these hernias can cause severe or fatal respiratory distress through so simple an act as the animal lying down on its side because there's nothing to keep organs in place.

Anal Atresia. There is no opening for the large intestine permitting the normal passage of stool.

Delayed Defects. The animal is born with defects but they may not be evident until later in life. Less than perfect heart valves and arterial problems are numbered among them. Signs these may be present in a kitten include less activity than the rest of its litter mates, stunted growth, and bluish interior lip membranes.

Cerebellar Hypoplasia. Quite often the result of a viral infection in the mother, kittens affected with it have a real locomotion problem. They're the unfortunate comedians of the litter due to a lack of development in the motor area of the brain, which causes staggering, lack of coordination, and too frequent rolling over. If the condition is not too severe, and if the cat is kept in a highly protective environment, the animal may adjust to its handicap.

Deafness. A color-linked defect, it occurs most often in pure white cats and is caused by a recessive gene.

Cryptorchidism. Often hereditary, this failure of one or both testicles to descend can cause tumors later in life. It's difficult for a lay person to determine in a young kitten and is usually discovered during an early visit to the veterinarian.

Brain Tumors. Causing pressure damage to a developing brain, some tumors may make their presence known immediately due to their effect on the central nervous system. Signs include loss of balance and confusion. See the section on Neurological Problems (pages 103-07) for additional information.

Liver Disease. One of the liver's tasks in life is to cleanse the blood of toxins. If the liver is unable to do so, these toxins build up in the blood and affect the brain. Signs of liver disease include seizures, stained teeth at four or five months of age, and darker, reddish urine. The ultimate result of liver disease is severe brain damage.

Colitis. This is an irritation to the lower bowel that can either be inherited or caused by a viral infection. If inherited, the causes can be neurological or allergenic. Chronic diarrhea is the result.

ADULT CAT OR KITTEN?

Due to their independent nature, cats are less adaptable than dogs, but your choice between a mature cat and a young cat should be based on your circumstances.

An older cat, two years and up, has a fully developed personality and a routine it prefers to follow. Whether you live alone or have a large family, you'll recognize how such a cat fits your life-style, and vice versa, very quickly. If you can establish the history of an older cat, it may be the best all-around bargain and present the least amount of problems.

However, if your desire to have a feline includes the opportunity for it and your children to grow up together, you will logically choose a kitten. Being a cat, and naturally fastidious, it will housebreak easily, but don't choose one less than seven to eight weeks old. By then, it will be eating on its own and be capable of escaping over-eager mauling at the hands of any toddlers in the house. Interplay between small children and small cats should be a parentally supervised event for more than just the cat's sake. Kittens have razor sharp claws that can cause serious damage to a child's face and permanent damage to the eyes. Those same claws will bear watching in defense of your furniture and all manner of other household property. They'll be used to poke, scratch, fray, climb, unravel rolls of bathroom tissue, cling to shiny door knobs, dig into potted plants, prance on newly polished surfaces and, occasionally, become stuck in the fine mesh of a screen door or window. There are few living things as adventuresome and curious as a kitten, and fewer that are more pure fun.

LONG HAIR OR SHORT HAIR?

Frankly, it depends on how much hair you want to clean up and how much time you're willing to devote to grooming.

With a short-haired cat, brushing once a week is enough. A long-haired cat should be groomed on a daily basis. If you don't do it, the cat will. And if the cat does it all the time, hair balls will collect in its stomach. Sometimes, the hair ball will be passed during the animal's natural processes of elimination. Sometimes, they are vomited up. But sometimes, hair balls get so large they must be surgically removed.

One other thing on the subject of short versus long hair. If you are slightly allergic to cats, but still want one, your allergy will be more tolerant of the short-haired variety because they naturally give off less dander.

INDOOR, OUTDOOR, OR BOTH?

Chances are, you're not going to allow your purebred Siamese, Angora, or Himalayan to wander around unattended in the outside world. As a matter of fact, you shouldn't. Even though they're all cats with natural predatory instincts and might survive, outdoor living is not for specialty breeds. For that reason, we'll limit life-style considerations to the domestic short hair.

Indoors, they'll live much longer and be exposed to far fewer perils, such as a neighbor's dog or trigger-happy youths with BB guns. If the outdoors surrounding your home is reasonably free of such things, however, the occasional presence of a cat stalking the property will liberate you from mice in the house and squirrels on the bird feeder. Admittedly, such peace of mind for you might be hazardous to the birds for which you erected the feeder, but in its ability to escape a domesticated cat, the bird is highly favored.

The purely outdoor cat is rare in populated areas. It's a cat whose owner wanted a cat, for whatever reason, but didn't want

---

NOTE: A cat that spends any time outdoors should be vaccinated for rabies. The disease is on the rise among felines and, in some areas, is approaching epidemic proportions.

---

the responsibility of owning one other than to provide it with food. But in a rural situation, such as a farm, food may be provided as a reward for services rendered. The cat knows it gets fed for keeping vermin out of the barn or grain, and it stays close to those areas even if it has reduced the pest population to zero. No sense messing with a good deal; not in the cat's mind.

NEUTERING? YES!

Neutering the female reduces the occurrence of mammary tumors and eliminates uteral diseases. Neutering the male prevents spraying, wandering, and fights, and increases companionability. When should your cat be neutered? Females at five months; males at seven months. If you know anything at all about cats, you know the cat population is exploding. The only, repeat, *only* reason not to neuter your cat is if you are intent on breeding it.

BEING ACQUIRED BY A CAT

It's easy. Just put food out for a stray. Cats, like hobos of the past, know which house is good for a handout. The word gets around, and if the stray you took pity on happens to be a queen, don't be surprised if you open your front door one day to discover one of her kittens deposited there. An infinite number of veterinarians have heard the words, "It's not my cat. I've only been feeding it." If you don't want to be acquired by a cat, you must have a heart . . . of stone.

ACQUIRING A PUREBRED CAT

Purebreds are also known as "specialty breeds." There's a two-and-a-half-inch-thick reference book that lists them, and it's getting thicker every day.

   Though you might obtain a purebred from other sources, if your heart's desire includes fine feline lineage, you'll be visiting a breeder. But remember this: the more finely bred the cat, the more susceptible it may be to any disease that comes down the pike. Some purebreds, due to congenital causes, are more subject to specific disorders than others. With any purebred, you can anticipate that special needs, special care, and special attention may be required. Follow the rule given previously, and take a new purebred cat to a veterinarian twenty-four to forty-eight hours after obtaining it. Having come from a breeder, the animal will most likely have a vaccination record and a history of any treatment given for, or to avoid, parasite problems. In addition, you should require the breeder to provide a certificate assuring you the cat is free from feline leukemia and infectious peritonitis, plus a guarantee against congenital problems. Be sure you accompany all of the above with a stool sample when you take the cat in for its checkup.

BREED-SPECIFIC HEREDITARY DEFECTS

These are more prevalent in purebred or pedigreed cats. Such animals are bred to enhance their good points, but the bad often comes with the good. We should note that most breeders are careful to monitor their breeding stock for signs of these defects, and, once discovered, to cull those parents out of the breeding line. However, some hereditary defects are not apparent early in life, and a kitten can be shipped out from one breeder to the next with neither party knowing the defect exists.

Siamese. Highly sensitive and more independent than the average cat, the Siamese is one of the most popular specialty breeds, but it is more prone to certain defects. Don't get turned off on Siamese because of what follows. They're great cats. Just be sure to get one without a hereditary defect. It won't be difficult. Most Siamese don't have any.

Among those defects is patent ductus arteriosis, involving a small artery that's supposed to fade away after birth. If it doesn't, it becomes entangled with and strangles the esophagus. Another is convergent strabissness or, to be blunt: cross-eyedness. Though not bred for it, some Siamese have it so badly they have trouble getting around.

A more serious problem, occurring in all cats, but more frequently with Siamese, results from the inability of the cartilage and bones to form properly. Cats so affected are stunted, have smaller ears in proportion to their head, a flatter and broader face with eyes set closer together, and may have bowed legs.

Persians and Angoras. Different colored eyes in these two specialty breeds are common and not at all life-threatening. However, the blue-eyed gene is associated with deafness.

Persians. These purebreds can have a complex metabolic problem which affects their ability to metabolize protein. Eventually, this causes neurological damage, signs of which can include loss of balance and an exaggerated, goose-step gait, and will ultimately weaken the heart muscle.

Abyssinians. Very finely bred cats, Abyssinians aren't too common and can inherit a protein metabolism problem that is totally different from the one found in Persians. It primarily affects the kidneys, causing depression, reduced activity, and dehydration.

TRAVELING WITH YOUR CAT

Most cats do not enjoy traveling. Too many new sights. Too many new sounds. Too many new smells. If you have any intention of taking Tabby along on your adventures, get Tabby used to the idea of being in a car early in life. Short trips around the block or to the store and back are a good way to start. For heaven's sake, don't let the only trips your cat takes with you be to a veterinarian, kennel, or groomer if you ever want it to accept the concept of going places. Convince the animal that getting into a car can result in a more pleasant, routine experience.

Remember, you're going to have to give up some of your time if you want to travel with your cat, and if you want your cat to consider traveling with you as something besides a disruption to be tolerated grudgingly, if at all. Part of that time should be spent making a checklist after thoroughly studying the following.

Pretrip Considerations. If you're traveling to a place the cat has never been before, call your veterinarian for an appointment a week to ten days ahead of departure to arrange for a general physical examination. Pretravel checkups are the best way to avoid problems arising along the way that you are ill-prepared to cope with or lack medication to treat. Don't wait until the last minute, because visits to the vet are stressful experiences for a good many cats. Give yours a chance to settle down for a few days before it has to face a car trip.

Pack along a little feline first aid kit. You might include tranquilizers, which you can secure from your veterinarian; the animal's medications, if any; first aid cream; a stomach-coating agent; and flea spray or shampoo.

We shouldn't have to remind you of this, but we will. Not all hotels, motels, or bed and breakfasts will accept animals as overnight guests. They're more apt to accept cats than dogs, though, and most apt to accept cats traveling in a carrier.

Some states and commercial carriers require health certificates for animals. Your veterinarian can tell you whether or not the state or states you're traveling to or through call for one. The commercial carrier you're using can tell you whether or not they require one, as well as providing you with their regulations for transport of the animal.

If you're traveling overseas, your cat may have to have certification by a federal veterinarian, which usually takes two weeks. (The name of a federal veterinarian can be obtained from your local vet.) Certification or not, some countries mandate a year's quarantine, and will actually take your cat from you upon arrival. You'll have visitation rights, and that's all. That's one reason you should check with the consulate of the country you're going to visit. Another reason for checking is to see if there's some weird cat disease going around over there which could require some special medication or vaccination.

Enroute. Be it a cardboard box or carrier, provide your cat with a den of its own when traveling. The animal will feel more secure and will be restrained, which is safer for both you and the cat.

An experienced feline traveler may move freely in and out of its den, causing no problems. With a new or somewhat unwilling voyager, there is the distinct danger of it taking up a position under the brake pedal or the driver's seat and refusing to budge until forcibly removed. With such animals, confinement to a carrier is recommended, and the carrier should be tied down so it won't fly around in case of a sudden stop or accident. If you can't bear the thought of confining your cat, *please* put a harness (not a collar) and leash on it and affix the leash to something in the car to restrict roaming. If you don't, the next tollgate you stop at could be the place your cat decides it's had enough and vanishes out your car's rolled-down window.

Don't be too concerned about confining your cat to a carrier. Cats were among the earliest practitioners of isometric exercise. They'll literally work out in the cage. In spite of this ability, do make provisions for exercise. You spend five hours in a car and need a stretch. So does your cat. Exercise also stimulates and maintains normal muscle function.

Feeding Enroute. Try not to feed your cat just prior to departure. About one-and-a-half to two hours before is better. Make it a light feeding, so the animal has a chance to digest it. While traveling, try to maintain a regular, twice-a-day feeding schedule. We recommend dry or semimoist cat food or small jars of baby food (beef, lamb, or chicken). Beware of canned food while on the road, because open cans spoil very easily, and consider bringing along a bottle or two of water from home which you can give the cat frequently and in small quantities.

Other Considerations. If your cat is used to a certain litter at home, bring the litter and the litter pan with you. There may be real problems otherwise, including bladder infections, because kitty can be reluctant to relieve itself in unaccustomed places.

Once you've arrived where you're going, don't turn the cat loose. It doesn't matter whether it's an indoor or outdoor cat: confine it to one area until it becomes accustomed to its new surroundings. When you've come back home, follow the same practice. A cat needs time to adapt, so give it the time it needs.

Cats Who Never Learn to Travel. Some find it so distasteful they simply can't adjust to it. Don't force the matter. Leave them at home, under the care of a responsible party, or place them in a reputable kennel. If you choose the latter, supply the kennel operator with the animal's favorite toy and the name of its veterinarian. No need to be very concerned about the cat being cooped up in a cage. If you remember what we've written about the cat's talent for isometric exercising, you know a period of confinement in a kennel isn't going to adversely affect muscle tone or function.

DIET

Cats have survived as they have by adopting the high-protein, high-fat, high-carbohydrate diet of a predator. Basically, this is the right diet for a young and middle-aged cat. But once your cat is weaned, there are so many really good commercial pet foods available that you can be assured your cat will receive a well-balanced diet simply by selecting a food it likes.

Most pet food companies recognize the differing dietary needs of cats according to age and formulate foods for every stage in the animal's life. You can trust the results developed by researchers of a recognized food company. Even veterinarians depend on their expertise as being superior, unless the vet specializes in nutrition. There are, however, certain general considerations.

A **newborn** normally gets everything it needs from its mother's milk. Cow's milk is not an acceptable substitute and can cause diarrhea in kittens because of the high sugar content. So when you're weaning a kitten and think it needs milk, use an orphan kitten milk supplement or facsimile available in a pet shop. At what age can a kitten be weaned? At about five weeks with canned or semimoist food given three or four times a day in small quantities. Once weaned, it will require three to four times the caloric intake of an adult cat, both to fuel its youthful exuberance and to encourage its growth during the critical first four to seven months of its life. The animal may need even more protein during this period. Your veterinarian can determine this and, if a dietary supplement is needed, your veterinarian can recommend one.

In **pregnancy**, a mother-to-be needs more protein to prevent deficiencies due the increased nutritional demands being made on her body. Your veterinarian will prescribe the one that's best for her. Don't try to pick a supplement off the shelf yourself. If you pick the wrong one it will do more harm than good. See the doctor!

If your cat is addicted to a special choice of food — Canadian sturgeon, Russian caviar, or white tuna chunks in water — the fault is yours. Your cat has you trained. But if your cat gets hungry enough, it will eat the most mundane cat food. It may sulk, but when its stomach says eat, eat it will.

Finally, there are specific dietary requirements for specific problems, such as FUS (feline urethral syndrome), diabetes, skin problems, and geriatric disorders. In such cases, veterinary diagnosis and dietary recommendations are the rule.

2

TRAUMATIC ACCIDENTS

Any accident can be traumatic, but all accidents aren't traumatic. Medically speaking—and we are—a trauma is a bodily injury: a wound, a broken bone, loss of skin and/or tissue. In other words, it's an emergency situation. In this section of the book, we'll identify specific traumatic injuries and describe what you can do to treat them on a first aid basis. In order to treat those injuries correctly, avoiding injury to yourself and further injury to your cat, pay close attention as you read this section.

Figure 1. A reasonably heavy cardboard box, large enough to easily accommodate the animal, will serve well in moving an injured cat to a veterinarian.

First, never be without a cardboard box of the appropriate size (Figure 1). With a folded towel or some other soft padding on the bottom, it is the ideal way to transport a traumatically injured cat to a veterinarian. At less critical times, it serves equally well as the place to which an injured cat can be confined while the animal heals.

MOVING AN INJURED CAT

Which brings us to Rule One: *If your cat is lying in the road, the first thing you must do is move the cat out of the road.* No exceptions. Not doing so only presents danger of further injury to your cat or injury to yourself. Of equal importance is Rule Two: *How you handle an injured cat depends on its mood after it's been injured.*

IS YOUR CAT UNCONSCIOUS?

If the cat isn't moving, doesn't respond to voice or touch, and its eyes are open and not focusing, you may safely assume it is unconscious. Pick it up by the scruff of the neck as shown to move it, or place it in a box and transport it to your veterinarian (Figure 2). Naturally, an unconscious cat is a cat with no objections to your administering first aid.

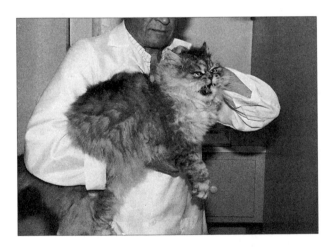

Figure 2. Place one hand under the animal's belly. Secure the front leg closest to your body with the same hand. At the same time, grasp the skin at the back of the neck with the other hand and lift to move the cat.

IS YOUR CAT CONSCIOUS AND FRIENDLY?

If the animal is conscious, allows you to touch, stroke, or gently handle it, and is not badly injured, you may pick it up. It's possible to transport your cat to your veterinarian in this manner, but placing it in the box, where it will feel more secure, is better. Just how friendly the cat feels at the moment will determine whether or not you will be able to give it first aid after you have moved it out of the way of further harm.

IS YOUR CAT CONSCIOUS, BUT UNFRIENDLY?

Not mad (we'll get to that), just unfriendly. The cat doesn't want to be touched and lets you know it. There's no opportunity to administer first aid in this case. You have to restrain your cat by wrapping it with a towel; then you can put it in the box and be on your way to medical help (Figure 3).

Figure 3. Place towel over cat and keep your hands behind the animal's head. Bring arms together, scoop up the cat and place in box.

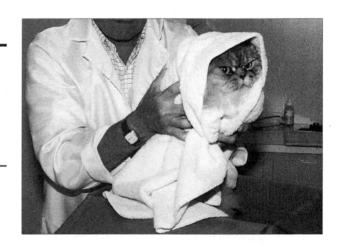

IS YOUR CAT CONSCIOUS AND ANGRY?

If so, it will not even allow you to put a towel around it, let alone administer first aid. You are now faced with the prospect of making the cat temporarily uncomfortable for its own good. Yes, what Figures 4A-C instruct you to do looks absolutely awful, but do it quickly and correctly and no harm will come of it.

There's another way of picking up a conscious and angry cat, but it only works if the cat's injury has immobilized it. You simply scoop the animal up with a shovel or other stiff object and gently deposit it in the box for transport (see Figure 5 on page 23).

RESTRAINING AN INJURED CAT PRIOR TO ADMINISTERING FIRST AID

Never attempt first aid without protecting yourself from being bitten. A cat's bite is one of the most infectious of all animal bites,

Figures 4A, 4B, 4C.
Using leash or rope
noose, slip it over the
cat's head (A). Extend
head forward by pulling
on the leash (B). At the
same time, grasp skin
over the hindquarters
with your free hand.
Lift cat quickly, but
gently, and lower into
box (C).

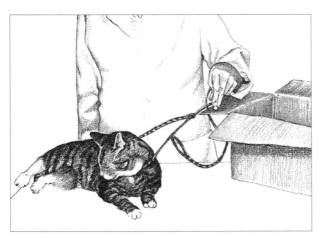

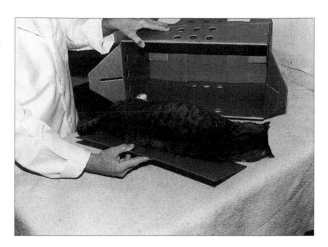

Figure 5. Place carrier or box on side. Then use stiff cardboard, a thin piece of plywood, or a shovel to scoop the animal in.

and once it's bitten into you, you're going to need medical attention *soon*. Just like the moray eel or monitor lizard, a cat may refuse to let go. In which case, you will wear it on your hand or arm until it has been tranquilized and has had its jaws forced open by a veterinarian.

There are muzzles available, used by cat care professionals, which are conical, cover the cat's head, and allow its nose to poke out. But you should forget muzzles unless you have one handy, know exactly what you're doing, and have had several dry runs at using it under the guidance of your veterinarian. Instead, use a towel or a shirt to cover the animal's head (Figure 6). If a cat can't see, it's a much calmer cat.

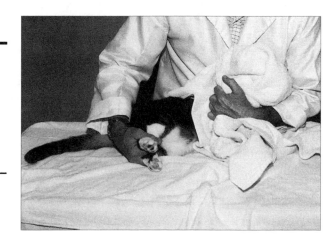

Figure 6. Place a towel completely over the animal's head. If you're treating an injury of the hindquarters, include the front feet in the wrapping process.

If you are attempting first aid on a head injury, you obviously can't cover the cat's entire head with a towel. Unless the injury is to the eye(s), you can use a strip of cloth or another towel as a blindfold, which should make the animal easier to handle while someone else helps you treat its head wound (Figures 7A, 7B).

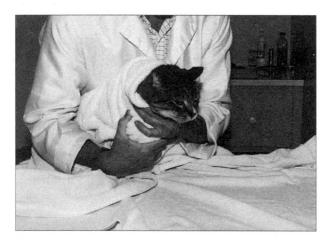

Figures 7A, 7B. Place cat on towel and wrap body (A). Use a corner of the towel or a separate, smaller cloth to cover the animal's eyes (B).

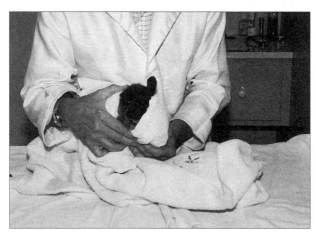

If the injury is to the eye, or eyes, wrap a bulky cloth around the cat's neck and grasp it firmly enough to hold the animal's head still (Figure 8). You may have to cover the eyes before you wrap the neck, then uncover them while you administer first aid. If so, be extremely cautious to avoid further injury. If you are faced with an angry cat, you must still pick up the animal and place it in a box for transport, but when a cat is mad, cover the *whole* animal before attempting to move it, as was shown in Figure 3 on page 21.

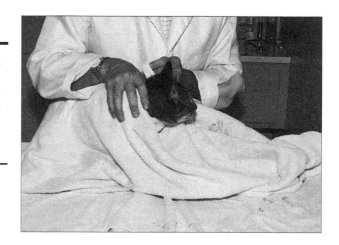

Figure 8. Place cat on a big towel. Wrap major portion of towel to cover neck and front feet. Use remaining portion to wrap or cover hind feet.

CATS AND CARS

Before we cover specific injuries resulting from a cat's encounter with a moving vehicle, we'll caution you about a feline's attraction to the car in your garage or parked in your driveway, usually your own car. Almost any injury a cat can suffer as a result of being struck by a car has been duplicated as a result of a cat having taken refuge under the hood, or in the wheel well, of a parked car. Keep that in mind before you next turn your key in the ignition. If you haven't seen Tabby around lately, double-check. Bang on the hood. Kick the tires. And always check underneath the car to see if the animal is lying there. It may be your automobile, but it's also part of your cat's home territory.

As for being hit by a car, if a cat can move after the impact it will bolt from the scene, and you're not going to find it. The animal is hurt and angry and hiding. If it survives, chances are it will limp home when it is able.

On the other hand, if the cat is unable to move after impact, immediately apply Rule One and *get the animal off the road*. Once that is done, you will have more time to evaluate the animal's injuries and determine what you may, or may not, be able to do to help.

SHOCK

During such an evaluation, there is a condition for which you should always be alert: shock. Any time a six- to nine-pound animal mixes it up with a ton or more of car, shock is a distinct possibility, regardless of the type of injury sustained. What is shock? Basically, it's a failure of the circulatory system. The blood is not being pumped to the tissues that depend on it, including the tissues of the brain. Therefore, the animal loses consciousness, and the heart itself may be in danger of failing due to insufficient blood supply. Besides loss of consciousness, other signs of shock are pale inner lip membranes, shallow breathing, and a decrease

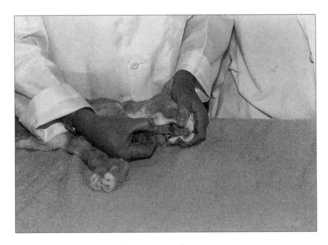

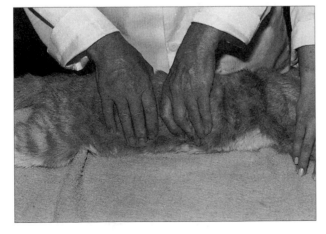

Figures 9A, 9B. Place cat on side with head extended. Pull tongue out to help maintain an open airway (A). To administer CPR, place both hands over posterior chest, then firmly and quickly press down / release every five seconds (B), until it becomes obvious the animal is not going to respond, or until you reach a veterinarian.

in body temperature. You don't need a thermometer to check the cat's temperature: the paws of the animal will feel cool to the touch and so will its mouth.

Treating Shock. Maintain an open airway. Make sure there are no obstructions in the mouth or nose to inhibit breathing. Position the cat so its head is extended, pull its tongue out to one side and administer CPR (Figures 9A, 9B). You won't have any trouble accomplishing all of the above because a cat in shock is an unconscious cat. You should also maintain the animal's body temperature with a blanket or hot water bottle, but don't overdo it. Too much heat applied to a cat in shock is almost as detrimental as not enough heat.

If there is external hemorrhaging, you'll have to set some priorities. Continued loss of blood will deepen the state of shock, but so will the lack of breathing. If you have to make a choice, get the animal breathing first, then worry about the bleeding. Hopefully, there will be someone nearby who can help, in which case you can accomplish both things at once.

If you're going to be delayed in getting the cat to a veterinarian, but the animal is semiconscious and is able to take fluids on its own, encourage it to drink something high in electrolytes — Gatorade, for example — or a solution such as salt and sodium bicarbonate formula.

SPECIFIC INJURIES

Simple Fracture, Leg. The detection of a simple fracture is fairly obvious. The leg has an angle that wasn't there before the accident occurred, but the skin isn't broken and no bone is protruding.

A simple fracture of the leg is not an emergency problem. We don't expect you to readily accept that statement, but it's true. However, the animal will be in pain. As long as the leg isn't badly broken, as in a compound fracture (see page 31), you can help. If your cat is amenable enough, or if you get to the scene of the accident while the animal is still stunned, you can gently straighten the leg. We said straighten it, not set it. Treat the leg as gently as possible.

If the accident has happened after veterinary office hours,

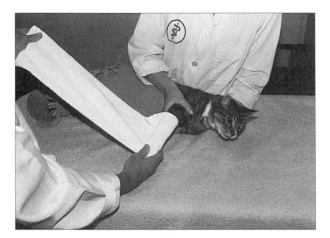

Figures 10A, 10B, 10C.
With injured leg held
extended (A), wrap a
towel, cotton wadding,
newspaper, or magazine
around it (B), and secure
it in place with a
bandage (C).

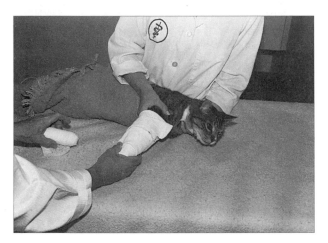

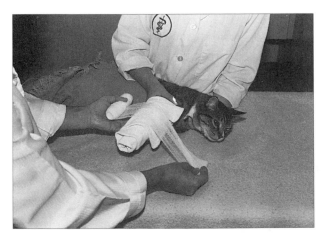

confine your cat in a box until morning. A cat with a broken leg isn't going to injure that leg further by dragging it around. A dog might, but not a cat. Most will simply curl up and think about it awhile.

If you're not going to be able to get your cat to a veterinarian within twenty-four hours, a simple restraining cast can be applied to the leg. You may use a roll of cotton or a rolled-up magazine or newspaper to maintain the leg in an approximately normal position. The procedure is demonstrated in Figures 10A-10C without head covering, which may or may not be necessary depending on the cat's temperament. You could do this alone, but having help always makes things easier.

Figures 11A, 11B. Use a belt, string, a piece of rope, or a strip of gauze to form loop around injured leg; tie a knot to maintain the loop (A). Insert a pencil, pen, or stick through the loop and twist sufficiently to stop the bleeding (B).

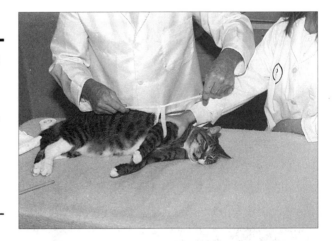

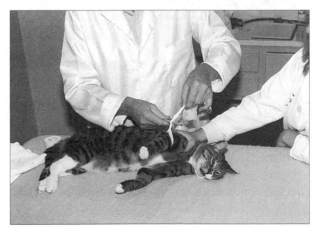

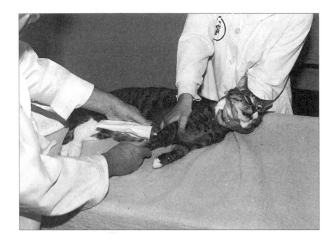

Figures 12A, 12B, 12C. After applying protective ointment (A), put a light bandage over the wound (B). Hold injured leg extended while you wrap a towel, magazine, newspaper, or roll of cotton around it (C), then secure in place with a gauze bandage.

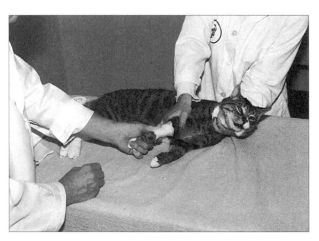

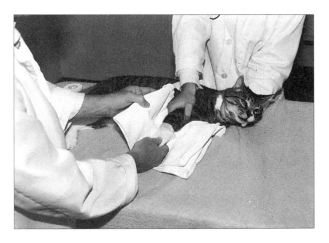

Compound Fracture, Fracture with Open Wound. Emergency treatment for both injuries is the same. An abnormal, often distressing, bend in the leg is obvious and is accompanied by an open wound. It may or may not be a compound fracture, in which case you would see the bone itself. If enough tissue has been lost, you may see the bone anyway.

Make no attempt to reduce the fracture by "setting the leg" yourself. If bleeding is not severe, place a clean, moist covering over the area to protect it. Something nonfibrous, such as a T-shirt. If there is serious bleeding, you're going to have to apply some sort of pressure *above* the fracture site to control it. You may do so with the simple tourniquet demonstrated in Figures 11A and 11B (see page 29).

Once the bleeding is under control, and if you are unable to secure immediate veterinary help, the wound must be further protected by the procedures shown in Figures 12A-12C. Apply petroleum jelly to the injured area, cover it, then immobilize the leg with a restraining cast and confine the animal in a box.

Fractured Tail. The cat is walking around, obviously in distress, hissing at people, and its tail is drooping. The animal can't seem to settle itself in a comfortable position and definitely doesn't want to be touched back there. All are signs of a fractured tail. There may or may not be swelling at the base of the tail.

There are only two things you can do to help if you can't immediately transport the animal to your veterinarian. One is to confine the cat so it can't further injure its already injured tail. Two is to give it an over-the-counter antihistamine tablet, which won't relieve the pain, but will to provide a mild sedative.

Whether or not the tail can be repaired depends on the amount of vascular and nerve damage that has been done. If such damage is severe, your veterinarian will probably recommend having the tail bobbed, which we think is wise. If you don't, the tail will always be in the cat's way, interfering with its bodily functions and generally making its life miserable.

Fractured Jaw. This is a frequent injury that is usually sustained to the lower jaw right underneath the chin. Quite often, there is little or no bleeding, and the injury is apparent because one side of the jaw is drooping. Should there be moderate or heavy bleeding, though, it's an indication the fracture is further back in the jaw.

With any jaw injury (and this is particularly true with a cat) there isn't much you can do in the way of first aid. What you can do you *must* do with extreme caution. If a lot of bleeding is present, pressure applied to the area will control or stop it (Figure 13). Use a cold, wet compress and an extra pair of hands, and avoid choking the animal or restricting its ability to swallow.

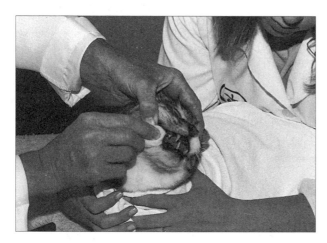

Figure 13. After wrapping the entire cat in a towel as demonstrated for head injuries, apply a cold compress to injured area with gentle pressure until bleeding subsides.

Fractured Spine. If the animal is attempting to get up on its front legs and its hindquarters are not functioning, it indicates an injury to the rear of the spine. Here again, first aid possibilities are limited. Your first concern is to prevent further damage with proper restraint and handling (Figures 14A-14C). If the injury is higher up on the spine, such as in the neck area, all four legs may not be functioning. Although more serious for the cat, restraint and handling is easier (see Figures 15A-15B on page 34).

Fractured Ribs. The cat will have a depressed chest. That is, the chest will have a "caved-in" appearance. First aid here consists of wrapping or bandaging the animal to restrict movement (see Figures 16A-16C on page 35). Not doing so could result in a fractured rib puncturing a lung, which would severely complicate matters. Be very careful and get someone to assist you, if possible. Remember, you're handling a small animal with small bones that could easily be further injured.

Figures 14A, 14B, 14C. Place cat on its side on a clean towel (A). Wrap entire body snugly, but not tight enough to impair breathing (B). Secure wrap in place with gauze bandage (C).

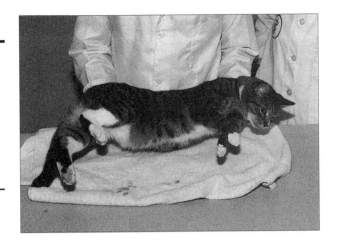

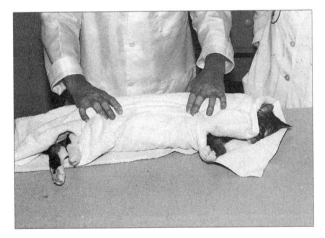

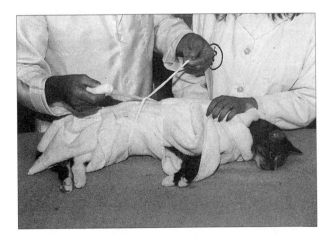

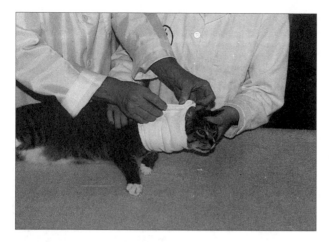

Figures 15A, 15B. Use a towel, roll of cotton, or folded T-shirt and wrap the cat's neck from chin to chest, being careful not to interfere with the animal's breathing (A). Secure wrap in place with bandage (B).

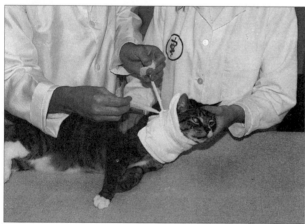

NOTE: With upper spinal fractures, the animal's ability to breathe may be impaired. If it is having difficulty breathing, you must, *very gently,* apply the technique for CPR as demonstrated in Figures 9A and 9B on page 26.

Large Lacerations (Little Bleeding). What's large? Anything over an inch. They can occur anywhere on the body and are usually accompanied by a surrounding numbness which makes first aid measures possible. Regardless of where these wounds occur, first check them to make sure they're clean. If there's going to be a delay getting to a veterinarian, use a sponge or clean, saturated

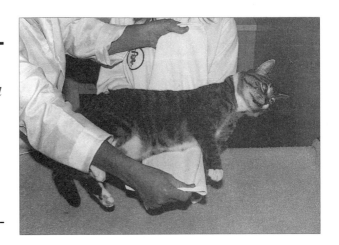

Figures 16A, 16B, 16C. Have an assistant pick up the cat on its side and slide a towel, roll of cotton gauze, or T-shirt underneath it (A). Wrap the chest gently (B), but not too loosely, and secure the wrap with a bandage (C).

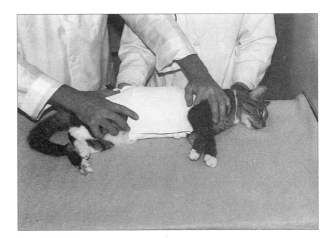

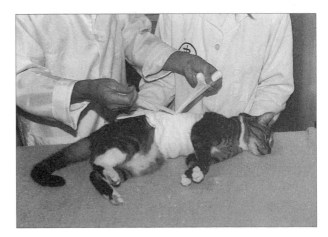

cloth to flush the wound with plain water. Encourage your cat to cooperate by covering its head, then clip the hair around the wound as shown and examine the injury for foreign matter (Figures 17A and 17B).

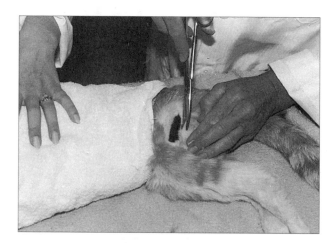

Figures 17A, 17B. After restraining the animal, flush the injury with plain water. Clip the hair around the wound (A), then use a cotton-tipped swab to remove any foreign debris trapped in it (B).

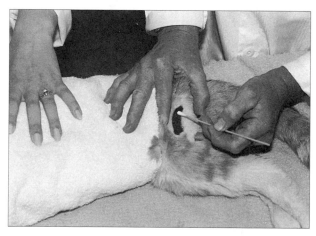

If there is dirt or other debris present which the flushing hasn't removed, you can use a cotton-tipped swab dipped in petroleum jelly to gently wipe out the worst of it. Once you have cleaned the wound to the best of your ability, or to the limit of your cat's patience, you should prevent the injured area from drying out too much. You can accomplish this by applying more petroleum jelly to the wound or by covering it with a clean, wet cloth. From here on, the only difference in treating a large laceration that isn't bleeding much from one that is bleeding is how you bandage it. And how you bandage it depends on where the bandaging needs to be done. Bandaging techniques for various body parts are shown in Figures 16 (body wounds), 18 (leg injury), and 19 (head wound).

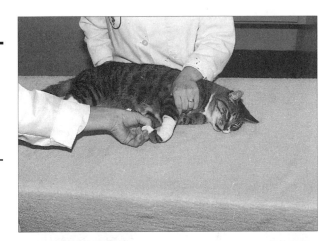

Figures 18A, 18B. Gently extend the leg, apply bandage over wound (A), and wrap with gauze to secure the bandage in place (B).

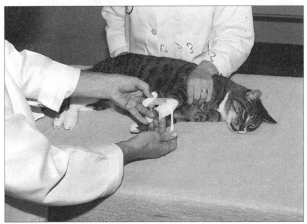

Large Laceration (Heavy Bleeding). The first priority is to quickly control the bleeding. You must apply direct pressure to the source of the bleeding, particularly if the wound is on the trunk. If the wound has occurred on an extremity, we still recommend direct pressure. If direct pressure doesn't work, apply a tourniquet as shown in Figures 20A and 20B on page 39.

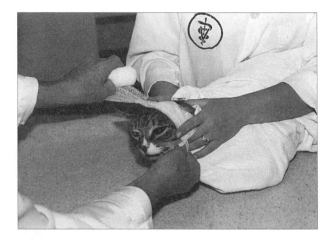

Figures 19A, 19B, 19C. Wrap body and legs in a towel, leaving only the animal's head exposed. Using a gauze bandage, wrap around the head to cover the injury (A and B) and secure the bandage to the head by tying it off as shown (C).

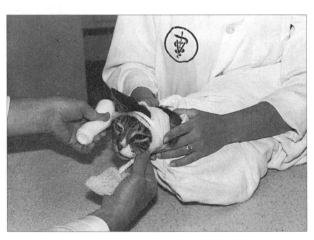

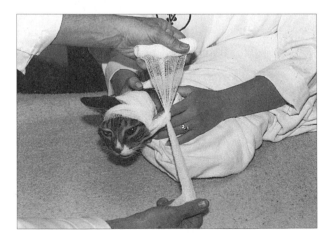

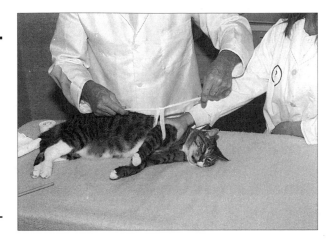

Figures 20A, 20B. Use a belt, string, a piece of rope, or a strip of gauze to form loop around injured leg; tie a knot to maintain the loop (A). Insert a pencil, pen, or stick through the loop and twist it sufficiently to stop the bleeding (B).

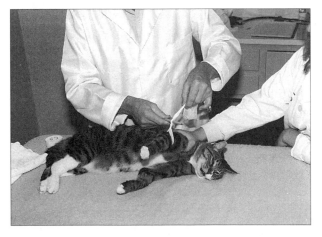

Once bleeding is controlled, flush the wound with clean water. If you use a wet swab to clean the wound further, don't probe too much. The more you probe such a wound, the more it will bleed. In addition, if there's a foreign body in there that gentle probing won't easily dislodge, it's best to leave it. Often, the presence of the foreign body itself prevents further bleeding. After you've stopped the hemorrhage, or feel you have it under control, you can apply a dressing, which will also serve as a pressure bandage.

IMPORTANT: Never remove a foreign body from a chest wound. It may have penetrated the chest cavity, lungs, or major blood vessels.

Bleeding from Mouth or Nose. If there is considerable blood coming from the mouth or nose, first aid is difficult, even if you have a cooperative patient. We recommend you make an attempt to keep the animal's head down. Most cats are smart enough to do this on their own, but if yours is particularly excitable and trying to struggle, run, get away, and keep breathing all at the same time, confine the animal in a box while trying to maintain the lowered head position.

If you're able to examine the mouth, you can check for a fractured jaw, a bitten tongue, teeth knocked loose, or a foreign body. It's not advisable to do much fussing around in a cat's mouth, though. Just try to clean out the mouth with some gauze to remove any large blood clots that the animal might swallow or choke on.

If the animal is alert and awake, you may gently flush the mouth out with plain water, but if the animal is unconscious, don't attempt it. It will cause choking. Sometimes, applying a cold cloth over the injured area will help reduce the bleeding, but use only a little pressure, and be sure to leave room for the animal to breathe (Figure 21).

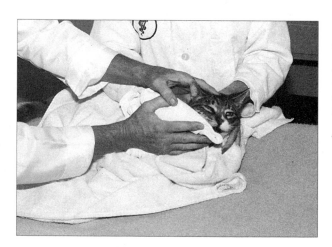

Figure 21. To reduce bleeding, gently apply a cold cloth over the site of the wound.

Since bleeding from the mouth or nose can be caused by a fractured skull, be prepared to transport your cat to your veterinarian as quickly as possible.

Minor Abrasion and Loss of Skin. Quite often, a cat will be dragged along by the car that struck it. The least that happens as a result is something like a burn. The hair is rubbed off, the skin is raw and oozing a bit. Such an injury is readily treated, no matter how large the area affected. If the area needs cleaning, flush it with water, then apply petroleum jelly or any mild first aid cream before covering the injury with a clean, wet cloth to protect it from further damage while you're on the way to your veterinarian. If the area that lost skin is clean, and they often are, you can skip the flushing.

Severe Loss of Skin. A complete layer of skin has been scraped off, revealing underlying tissue. There will be bleeding, but not very much in most cases. If the wound needs cleaning, flush it out with cold water to remove the most obvious debris. Apply petroleum jelly or first aid cream, cover with a clean, wet cloth, and get the animal to your veterinarian.

NOTE: When, in addition to great loss of skin, there is moderate to heavy bleeding, refer to the section, **Large Laceration (Heavy Bleeding)** on page 37, and follow procedures given to control the hemorrhaging.

Severe Loss of Skin and Tissue. Here the injury has been severe enough to have removed actual muscle tissue and perhaps affected the underlying bone. Though obviously a more serious injury, first aid treatment doesn't differ significantly from that recommended for severe loss of skin, but here you may be faced with the additional complication of a fracture or exposed joint.

Excessive flushing is not recommended, since it may actually flush dirt into joint cavities. The best measure is to protect the wound with a clean, wet cloth and take the cat to a veterinarian. If you also discover a fracture of an extremity or joint, it should be immobilized with a heavy bandage to prevent further damage.

Eye Injury (Bruised Exterior). What this amounts to is a "shiner." There is considerable swelling around the eye and of the eyelid.

There may be so much, in fact, that you will be unable to see the globe of the eye itself.

If you're fresh on the scene, take a cold cloth, restrain the animal, and hold the cloth over the eye (Figure 22).

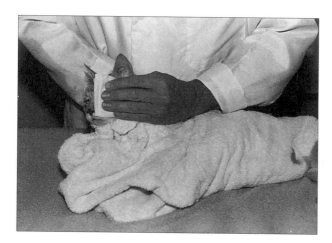

Figure 22. Wrap a towel or T-shirt around the cat's neck and body. Hold it gently but firmly to immobilize the animal's head, and protect yourself while you're applying a cold compress to the eye.

Eye Injury (Laceration of the Eyelid). A bruise to the eye may or may not be accompanied by a cut eyelid. Flush the area with artificial tears or an over-the-counter eyewash solution. If you don't have such things handy, the cut must still be flushed out and you can use plain water to do it. If there's a lot of bleeding, apply a cold compress. Once the bleeding is under control, you can apply plain petroleum jelly or a nonprescription eye ointment to the area.

Eye Injury (Scratched or Cut Eyeball). It is quite possible to scratch or cut the surface of the eye without imposing on the integrity of the eyeball. If you are able, flush the eye with artificial tears or commercially available eyewash and place a cold compress over the eye. Your cat will close its eye when you apply the compress, which is okay. The lid over the eye will provide better protection to the injury than you could provide.

If the cat is conscious, or feeling uncooperative, you will have to restrain it to prevent it from pawing at its eye and aggravating the injury.

Eye Injury (Rupture or Out of Socket). The treatment is the same for both. Restrain the cat. Do nothing except protect the eye with a clean, moist, lint-free cloth. An eye so seriously injured can still be saved, but there's nothing you can do to save it except to confine your cat and transport it immediately to your veterinarian. Repeat: *immediately.*

Internal Bleeding (Subsurface Bruises). This is internal bleeding in its simplest form. You cat is black and blue in addition to whatever other color, or colors, it happens to be. There is no external bleeding, no oozing of fluid. Such injuries are simple to treat, even though they may be extensive. The bruise will be apparent due to swelling, and the area will be rather sensitive for the animal. Apply cold compresses to the affected area regularly for twenty-four hours. If no lessening of the swelling is detectable after that period of time, call your veterinarian.

Internal Bleeding (Chest and Abdomen). These, of course, are the most serious forms of internal bleeding. There may be no external injury to indicate that your cat is experiencing internal bleeding, but there are signs to look for. Blood may be passing from the nose or mouth. Your cat may cough or vomit up blood. Blood may pass out with the stool. Your cat's inner lip membranes will be pale if there is loss of blood, and the animal will obviously be in a weakened condition. Check for shock as described at the beginning of this chapter. If those signs are present as well, follow the procedures given and quickly secure veterinary help.

Evisceration (Minor). It may sound oxymoronic to address any rupture of the abdominal wall as "minor," but, in this case, the internal organs are still contained within the body. You will notice a swelling or distension of the skin. It will be large and soft and sensitive. There is no first aid treatment you can apply, so confine the animal and be on your way to your veterinarian.

Evisceration (Major). Here, both abdominal wall and skin are ruptured and you're facing a very unpleasant sight. The cat's internal organs are lying there, outside the body. What you must do isn't first aid, but if your cat is to survive, you must do it and do it quickly (see Figures 23A-23C, next page).

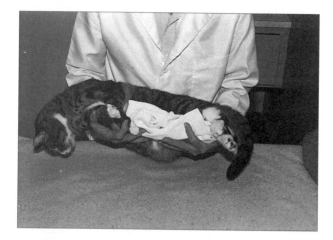

*Figure 23A, 23B, 23C.
Gather the exposed
internal organs together
(A). Holding the organs
close to the cat's body,
place them and the
animal on a wet towel or
T-shirt (B) and snugly
wrap both organs and
animal in a single pack-
age for transport (C).*

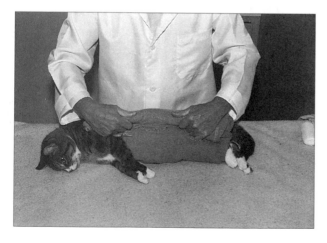

Open Chest Wound. The primary problem to be solved from a first aid standpoint is to maintain respiration. You must cover the offending wound as quickly as possible with a clean, wet cloth. Once covered, a pressure bandage will be needed to keep the cloth in place (Figures 24A, 24B). With the bandage in place, you may have to assist and encourage your cat's breathing by administering CPR, which was shown in Figures 9A and 9B on page 26.

Figures 24A. 24B. Place a wet towel or T-shirt over the open wound (A). Secure it in place with several wraps of gauze bandage (B).

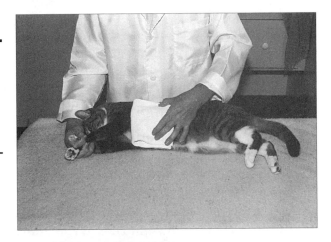

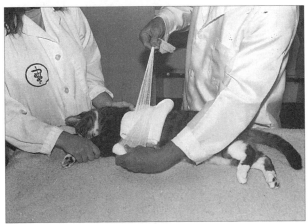

OTHER CAT-TASTROPHES

We're still dealing with trauma. There's a wound, an injury to some part of the body, or a burn that just happened which, in most cases, is treatable on a first aid basis. At this point, either remember or reread everything stated previously in regard to restraint, confinement, and transport of an injured cat. If it seems like we're harping on pretty basic stuff, you're absolutely correct. Unless the first steps you take in trying to help your injured cat are the right steps, you'll injure it further or get injured yourself. We could identify a number of people who bear the scars of making the wrong approach to an injured feline. Worse, we could tell about literally hundreds of cats that didn't survive an accident, but could have, if their owners had known and remembered what to do first. We prefer not to; we'd rather harp.

You're going to be upset if and when any of the following misfortunes befall your cat. No matter how upset you are, it is critical to remember the basics before you do anything else.

Flights of Fancy. The launching pads for these short, jarring jaunts can be a tree limb, terrace, fence, or the sill of an open window.

The purpose of the leap can be escape or pursuit or combat. Something or someone has frightened the cat. Something, perhaps a bird, has attracted the cat. Something, usually another cat, has dared to set foot on what the cat considers its turf. "And away we go!" as Mr. Gleason used to say. Unfortunately, there is no humor to be found at this journey's end, and, if the fall came from a sufficient height, no first aid procedures will apply. The cat will be dead.

Now, let's look at the brighter side of flights of fancy, and the ways you can help a cat that has taken one. It's very true that cats land on their feet. But when they land on their feet after leaping from high places, their momentum slams their chin and chest against the ground.

Flights of Fancy (Injured Chin and Jaw). Impact has split the bottom jawbone. Quite commonly, the skin has been peeled back off the jaw from the point of the chin. Among veterinarians, the injury is known as "the high-rise syndrome." It's dreadful looking, but if treated promptly it heals quite nicely.

Chances are very good the cat will be stunned, if not unconscious, which makes administering first aid somewhat simpler if there's going to be a delay getting medical help. You'll only have two or three minutes to work with before the cat will regain its senses enough to be mad at the world, so act quickly or don't act at all.

You can't tug the loose skin forward completely, but you can reposition it enough to cover at least part of the injury. The part of the wound that is still exposed can be protected by gently smearing it with petroleum jelly. After doing so, confine the cat and transport it to your veterinarian, where final repairs can be made.

Flights of Fancy (Compressed Chest). This injury often accompanies the split and peeled jaw. If the cat is unconscious or semiconscious and in severe respiratory distress, you may place it on its side and very gently apply CPR. There could be internal damage, so any roughness on your part will only worsen the condition. Be careful! Naturally, the sooner the animal receives veterinary care the better.

Animal Bites (Cat Bites Cat). The most common animal bite your cat will receive will come from another cat. It is also the most serious and the most subject to infection.

A cat's fangs are small and razor-sharp; they carry enormous amounts of bacteria, and create a very small entry wound. Once the fang has punctured the skin, however, it makes a tearing, ripping wound beneath it: a perfect incubator for bacteria that were on the skin and teeth to develop into a very nasty abscess.

Let's first assume that you know your cat has just been bitten by another cat. What can you do from a first aid standpoint? You should first restrain the animal, then clip the hair away from the punctured area, flush it with clean water, wash it with mild soap and water, then flush it with hydrogen peroxide (see Figures 25A and 25B, next page). If you can, swab the injury with a little petroleum jelly or first aid cream.

The secret to success in keeping infection out of the wound is to keep the wound open, clean, and scab-free. In the case of a bite, swab it *daily* with petroleum jelly or first aid cream, to allow the wound to heal from the inside out (see Figure 26, next page).

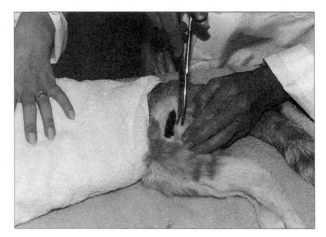

Figures 25A, 25B. After restraining the animal, flush the injury with plain water. Clip the hair around the wound (A), then use a cotton-tipped swab to remove any foreign debris trapped in it (B).

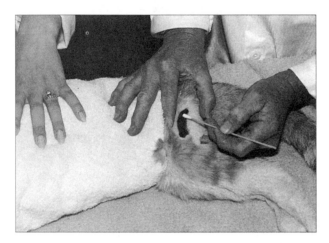

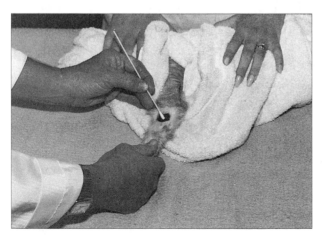

Figure 26. To make sure a wound heals from the inside out, swab it daily with petroleum jelly or first aid cream.

Now let's assume that you didn't see your cat get bitten. A major problem with a cat bite is that the initial puncture wound is so small and is covered by hair. The owner is often unaware that his or her cat has been bitten until the animal shows some signs after the fact. These include limping, swelling, or sensitivity in an area of the body that wasn't sensitive before. Be watchful for these signs because, if you miss them, you'll soon be faced with a draining abscess. Quite frequently, there is blood mixed in with the purulent matter.

Do you have an emergency on your hands? Not as much of one as it might first appear.

First, flush the bite area with clean, cold water to get rid of any surface deposits from the discharge. Next, very gently press around the area to encourage additional emission of the discharge. Once you feel you've gotten as much discharge out of the abscess as your cat will allow, and you can see the infected area, clip the hair around it. Flush with hydrogen peroxide and swab the wound with a mild first aid cream. Refer to the immediately preceding series of photos and instructions on how to keep the wound open during the healing process.

Sometimes, one of these larger wounds is close to a joint. It may then be advisable to put a temporary splint and dressing over it to prevent the cat's movements from reopening the wound and to protect it from further injury.

CAUTION: If, after clipping, you discover an extensive infection surrounded by a large patch of discolored skin you should immediately seek veterinary help and not attempt to treat the wound further yourself.

Animal Bites (Dog Bites Cat). These are also puncture wounds, but the teeth that made the punctures are much larger and cause much more tissue damage. If the laceration is *small*, flush it with cold water to remove surface debris. You then may probe the wound gently with a swab to cleanse it further. Flush again, this time with hydrogen peroxide, then apply a mild first aid cream. Remember to keep the wound open so it heals from the inside out.

If the laceration is *large*, and there is considerable bleeding, flush it with cold water and apply a cold, wet compress in an effort to bring the bleeding under control. If you're successful, you may then do a *little* probing of the interior of the wound to remove debris. Wipe the area with a pad soaked in hydrogen peroxide, apply first aid cream or petroleum jelly, and be on your way to your veterinarian. If you haven't totally controlled the bleeding, you'll have to keep pressure on the injured area with a clean cloth while someone else drives you and the cat to the vet.

NOTE: With large bite wounds, be alert for signs of shock and internal injuries. The dog may have picked up the cat and shaken it during the attack. There may be a tremendous amount of damage beneath the bite area itself. Be prepared to treat the cat for shock and for chest or abdominal injuries, and waste no time securing medical help.

Animal Bites (Snake Bites Cat). Though not too common, they do happen, and the degree of danger the cat is in depends on the kind of snake that bit it.

If it was a poisonous snake, there will be four small puncture wounds. If it was a nonpoisonous snake, there will be a U-shaped pattern on the skin. If you're sure your cat has been bitten by a nonpoisonous snake, treat the wound as you would a minor laceration. Wash with mild soap and water, wipe with a hydrogen-peroxide-soaked cloth, and apply first aid cream.

If you spot the punctures, you can be reasonably certain the bite carried snake venom with it, and that the poison has entered the cat's body. First, wash the wound with mild soap and water. In treating a cat bitten by a poisonous snake you don't have to orally suck out the poison, but you will definitely have to restrain the animal.

Once you have restrained the animal, apply cold compresses (an ice pack is ideal) to the affected area to reduce circulation and prevent the poison from spreading. Encourage bleeding around the puncture marks as shown in Figures 27A-27C to flush venom from the wound. And please, with *any* snake bite, get your cat to a veterinarian as soon as possible.

*Figures 27A, 27B, 27C.
Restrain the cat by
wrapping its head and
as many unaffected legs
as you can in a towel (A).
Using a sharp
implement — we're
demonstrating with
forceps here — enlarge
both fang holes to
encourage bleeding (B).
Apply a tourniquet above
the bite wound (C).*

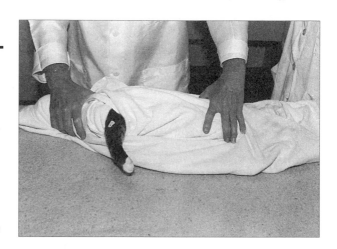

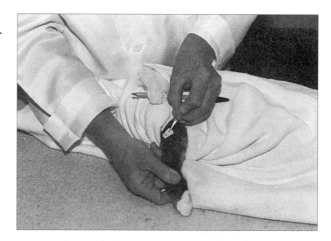

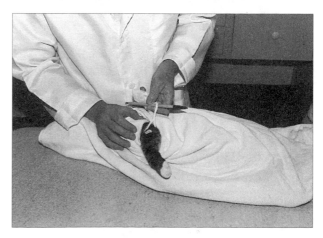

Puncture Wound to Skin (Caused by a Foreign Body). The cat has run into or stepped on something, and the foreign body that caused the wound is not stuck in the wound. All puncture wounds of this type are initially treated pretty much the same way. Clean the area with mild soap and water, apply direct pressure to control any bleeding, cleanse the wound itself gently with more soap and water, and apply a mild, antibiotic first aid cream or petroleum jelly. You may wish to protect the injury further with a light dressing before transport to your veterinarian. If so, a gauze pad held in place with a two or three wraps of gauze bandage will do nicely (Figures 28A, 28B).

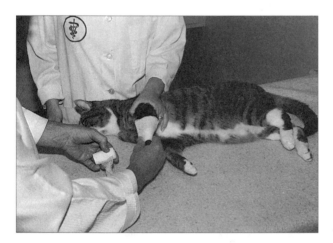

Figures 28A, 28B. Place a sterile gauze pad or clean, folded cloth over the wound and hold it there (A). Keep the pressure on while you wrap it with gauze strips to keep it in place (B), then wrap everything you've done with more gauze to secure it.

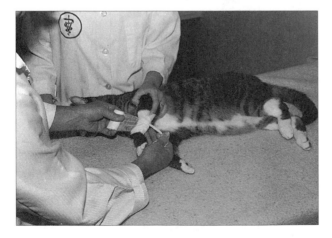

If the wound is large or deep, we recommend no more in the way of first aid than just described, but urge as little delay as possible in getting medical help.

Puncture Wound to Eye (Caused by a Foreign Body). Any time anything punctures your cat's eye, the eye is going to get the worst of it. Another cat's claw is the most common cause, but a twig or similar sharp object has the same effect. Because such wounds are often self-sealing, you may not be aware of the injury for two or three days. After that period of time, there will be no mistaking the signs. The eye will have become infected and will be tearing. The animal will blink a great deal and be obviously unhappy. If you

Figures 29A, 29B. Restrain the animal by having someone else wrap its body and legs in a towel or small blanket. Place your thumb under the cat's chin and your index finger on its upper eyelid. Use your index finger to hold the eye open and a soaking wet cloth, sponge, or paper cup full of clean water to flush out the eye (A). After flushing, use the thumb and index finger combination to hold the eye open while you use an eyedropper or squeeze tube to apply drops or eye ointment to the corner of the eye (B).

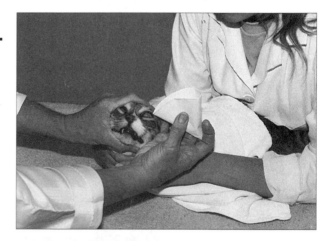

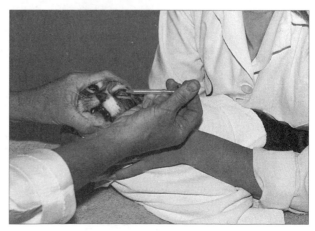

can't get medical help immediately, flush the eye with any non-prescription eyewash you may happen to have on hand. If you have no eyewash, use warm water (Figures 29A, 29B). Once you've washed out the eye, apply a drop or two of mineral oil to soothe the injury.

You should also know that a mild eye ointment prescribed by an opthalmologist for use in a human eye is perfectly safe to use in a cat's eye and will likely be of more benefit than the suggested mineral oil. It won't eliminate the need for veterinary attention, though, and the sooner your cat gets to the doctor, the better.

Puncture Wound to Skin (Foreign Body Retained). Whatever was run into, stepped on, or rolled on has penetrated the skin and hasn't come out. How you treat the resulting wound depends on the foreign body that caused it.

1. Small Foreign Body. A thorn, a splinter, a small sliver of glass, for example, or a grass awn. What's a grass awn? It's the sharp, little point at the end of a blade of grass wherein lies the seed. Though insignificant in size, these and other small foreign bodies are notoriously sneaky.

Chances are very good that the cat's owner won't know the object has penetrated the cat's skin until the animal begins to lick or "worry" the affected area with some frequency. Once such behavior is noted, a further examination will usually reveal a pimple-like abscess indicative of something being in there. For heaven's sake, your sake, and your cat's sake, don't go probing for it. Wash the area with mild soap and warm water, accompanied by brief, very mild squeezing of the pimple, two or three times a day. Hopefully, it will break and drain. Moisten a gauze pad with hydrogen peroxide and gently dab it on and around the draining abscess. If the process of draining and sterilization with the peroxide is successful, the wound will heal without further treatment being necessary. If the foreign body remains within, the abscess will reoccur, and a veterinarian will have to surgically remove it.

2. Large Foreign Body. It's so obvious you can't miss it. It's sticking right out of your cat's body. *Don't try to pull it out!* If you can cut it off two to three inches from the point of penetration, fine.

Whether you'll even be able to do that is doubtful, since your cat's frame of mind will likely be at its most foul. There is nothing, absolutely nothing, further you can do from a first aid standpoint in these cases. It's best for all concerned if you simply confine the cat to a box or carrier and seek veterinary help immediately.

3. Porcupine Quills. Evidently cats have far more respect for Mr. Porcupine than dogs do because we've seen few felines wearing the quills of a close encounter. But it can happen, and if you and your cat are in an area where you can't get veterinary help for two or three hours, you'll have no choice but to remove the quills yourself (Figures 30A, 30B). Your cat won't like it. Neither will

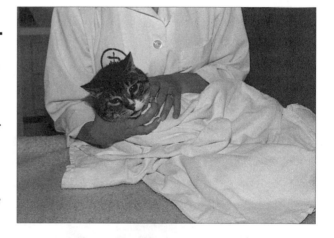

Figures 30A, 30B. Wrap a towel around the cat to secure all four feet (A). With a helper immobilizing the animal's head, use a pair of needle-nose pliers to firmly grasp the quill as close to the skin as possible (B). **Don't pull straight out**. *Rotate the quill right and left as you pull steadily. A quick pull might break off the quill.*

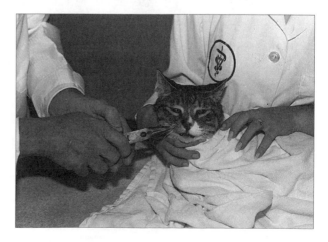

you. You're going to need help, and you're going to have to do the removing fast.

Secure the animal, leaving the quill-carrying area exposed. Use needle-nosed pliers if available. If they're not available use any kind of pliers. Lacking those, use gloves, a piece of steel wool, or anything that's going to give you a firm grip.

WARNING: The tips of porcupine quills can easily break off when the quill is being removed and remain inside the cat. Weeks, even months later, a foreign body reaction to the quill tip will result in an open, draining wound. Worse, these tips will migrate internally for inches, not millimeters, and require surgical removal. No matter how good a job you think you've done to rid your cat of quills, see your veterinarian as soon as possible.

---

4. Fish Hooks. If you've just brought a pole back from a fishing trip, perhaps with a bit of worm still attached to the hook, it may prove too great a temptation for your cat to resist. Ever curious, ever venturesome, the cat may, indeed, find itself the catch of the day.

No matter where your cat gets itself hooked, leave the hook alone. You can't pull it out, and no conscious cat is going to allow you to try and push it through. Cut the line, confine the animal to a box or carrier, and get immediate medical help. If you can't reach your veterinarian or the veterinarian on call, head for the nearest veterinary emergency clinic. There is nothing, absolutely nothing, you can do as an alternative.

Puncture Wound to Eye (Foreign Body Retained). The foreign bodies we're concerning ourselves with here are of the smaller variety. In most cases, their invasion of the eye isn't all that painful after the initial shock, and the animal will be quite complacent. Make no attempt to remove the object. Cover both the animal's eyes with a clean, cold, moist cloth. Keep the cat's complacency working for you by confining it, then get the two of you to your veterinarian.

Foreign Bodies in Ear. Cats, unlike dogs and other animals with large, floppy ears, aren't plagued by objects sticking into their ears. However, the hunter cat might arrive home with a grass awn, a seed, or a tick in its ear. If so, that animal will be very unhappy. There will be much shaking of the head and almost as much rubbing of the ear along the rug or floor.

If you notice the behavior immediately, and can see the foreign body (and see that it's not imbedded), you may be able to remove the problem with a cotton-tipped swab or pair of tweezers. (Figures 31A, 31B).

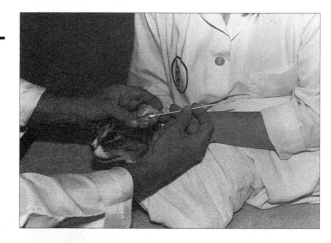

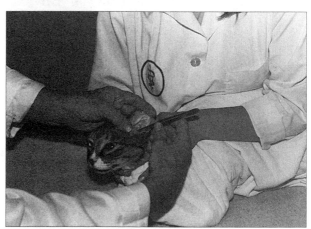

Figures 31A, 31B. Have whomever is assisting you wrap the body securely and immobilize the animal's head. If you're using a cotton swab, gently probe for and attempt to wipe out the foreign body (A). If you're using tweezers, grasp the foreign body and remove it, unless it's a fish hook (B).

If you miss the signs described above, the ear will become very inflamed within two to three days. Inflammation will be accompanied by a fluid discharge. Make no attempt to remove the bothersome object — your cat won't put up with it. A few drops of mineral oil in the ear will help soothe the irritation while you confine the animal and take it to your veterinarian.

Puncture Wound (Gun Shot). Unfortunately, we see a large number of cats with so-called "cold" gunshot wounds, caused by an air rifle in the hands of a very uncaring or irresponsible person. Cats seem to be an easy and attractive target for young, would-be marksmen. Be alert for any such youngsters that happen to live nearby and keep your cat indoors when you suspect such hunters are on the prowl.

The BB shot wound can be troublesome, because the projectile is not sterile when it penetrates the skin. As a result, the projectile behaves like any dirty, foreign body and causes infections. It's very likely you won't be aware that your cat has been shot; the wound is small and the animal's fur will prevent it from being easily seen. You will more likely realize that something is wrong when a lameness or festering appears, unless the injury has been caused by one of the larger caliber, pellet-type air rifles. In which case, there may be a fractured bone, a spinal injury, and/or paralysis, and the cat will require immediate veterinary care.

If you discover the initial BB shot wound, treat it as a puncture wound: Clip the hair around it, wash with mild soap and water, then apply hydrogen peroxide and first aid cream. *Do not attempt to probe for the BB shot.* That's strictly a job for your veterinarian.

The other type of gunshot wound, resulting from a rifle or shotgun, causes a tremendous amount of instantly apparent initial damage. Such a wound from a rifle is almost always fatal. But, if the firearm used was a shotgun and the shell contained a charge of bird shot, the cat has a chance. In the first place, the wound is sterile; great heat is generated in the barrel of a shotgun. The pellet or pellets that enter the cat are also hot. As they enter, they actually sterilize the wound they cause. If the pellet enters a noncritical area, you can treat it as a large puncture wound. Clip the hair, wash the area, and apply hydrogen peroxide and first aid ointment. A light dressing should be employed to protect the injury while you're on the way to a veterinarian.

If it's any comfort, cats have been struck by a solid point, .22 caliber bullet and survived. In all cases, the bullet entered and exited the body without hitting anything vital on the way through. There is very little the owner can do in such cases, other than applying pressure to arrest bleeding of the obvious wound while being alert for signs of shock and internal injuries and getting the animal quickly to a veterinarian.

Ear Injury (Torn or Bitten). The most common injury to a cat's ear or ears results from a battle with another cat. There will always be a lot of bleeding. Your first concern is to control it. Apply pressure to the ear with a cold, damp cloth or sponge for ten minutes to be sure the bleeding has stopped. If the cat insists upon undoing what you have accomplished by shaking its head or pawing at the injury, both of which will start the bleeding anew, you will have to protect the ear to promote healing by covering it with a dressing (see Figures 32A-32C, next page).

Ear Injury — Hematoma. Due to a blow, pinch, or mild bite, the blood vessels under the skin of the ear have been ruptured, leaving no external wound. Since there's no way out for the blood, it collects under the skin as what is commonly called a "blood blister." The ear will be swollen and look like a small pillow. Though not exactly an emergency, it's still very annoying to the cat, and the treatment is solely to prevent further damage. Do not puncture the hematoma in an attempt to drain it or reduce the swelling. Secure the ear with a dressing as shown in Figures 32A-32C, and limit the animal's ability to scratch at its head by placing it in a box or cat carrier. It's amazing how quickly a cat will settle down and begin its healing process when it has been confined to a small area.

Nose Injury (Cut). Any cut to the nose will result in a lot of bleeding. Apply pressure to the cut itself with a cold compress. Once the bleeding is under control, wipe the area with a cloth, sponge, or gauze pad that has been dampened — not soaked — with hydrogen peroxide. Then apply a mild first aid cream or ointment.

Nosebleed. Applying pressure with a cold compress over the bridge of the nose can help. A cat doesn't take kindly to such measures,

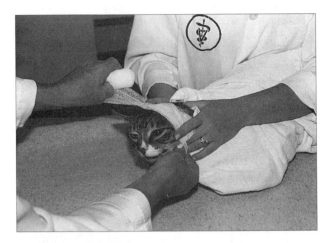

Figures 32A, 32B, 32C. Wrap body and legs in a towel, leaving only the animal's head exposed. Using a gauze bandage, wrap around the head to cover the injury (A and B), and secure the bandage to the head by tying it off as shown (C).

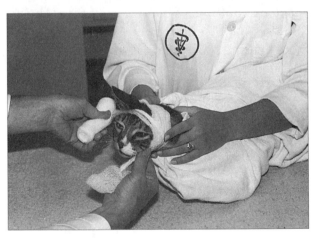

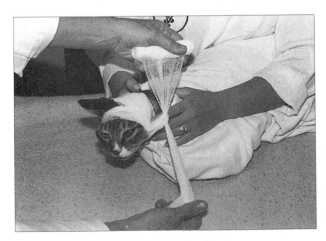

though, so all you may be able to do is confine it to a small space. The less the cat can move around, the sooner the blood will clot.

Nose Injury (Caused by a Foreign Body). It's rare, but it happens. A cat will run into something, and that something will enter into and stick in a nostril. If you believe you can easily remove the object, restrain the cat, pull out the foreign body (Figure 33) and transport the animal to your veterinarian.

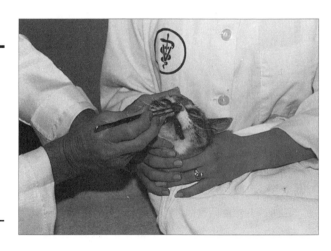

Figure 33. Secure all four legs in a body wrap and have an assistant hold the animal's head still. Using forceps or tweezers, firmly grasp the foreign body. Turn your hand **clockwise** *as you pull steadily and quickly.*

Burns, General. If there's anything madder than a wet hen, it's a burned cat. It doesn't matter whether the burn is caused by a spilled pot of boiling water, paw pads on hot asphalt, a stroll on a stovetop that was cool only minutes before, or by contact with a flame. If your cat can move after the pain begins, he or she will be long gone, and woe to the owner who attempts to dislodge it from the place it's chosen to hide until the hurt goes away.

If you're cat is burned, getting it to cooperate while you try to administer first aid is going to be your biggest problem. Unless the animal is seriously burned, you'll have to restrain it. We'll tell you why that's true a little later. Right now, it's best that you become familiar with the different types of burns caused by heat.

The least serious is a *first-degree burn.* They're very superficial. The skin is red, like a sunburn, but there's been no damage to hair follicles. Unless the burn has been caused by an open flame, there will be no singed hair.

The *second-degree burn* does greater damage to the skin. It's greatly inflamed. Blisters have developed, and there is a moist, post-burn seepage of body fluid. If the burn was fire-related, singed hair will be very apparent, the follicles will most likely have been destroyed, and the cat's hair can be easily pulled out by the handful. Not a pleasant thought, but a sure sign of a second-degree burn.

The *third-degree burn* results in serious skin, even tissue, loss. There is blackened charring of the skin surface, severe damage to hair and hair follicles. It's ironic, but the worst kind of heat burn a cat can suffer is the easiest to treat from a first aid standpoint, because the animal will be either semiconscious or totally unconscious.

Heat Burns, First- and Second-Degree. If you're immediately aware that the animal has been burned, douse the burned area with cold water. Plenty of it. This will lower the temperature of the affected area and will prevent it from "cooking" further. It will also reduce the pain.

How do you restrain a burned cat while you douse it with cold water? Use a wet towel or T-shirt. Cast it over the cat like a net,

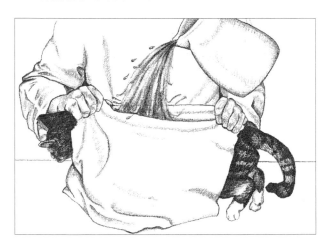

Figure 34. Wrap animal in a wet towel or T-shirt, keeping the head free. Pour cold water on the cloth. Really pour it on. The sooner you get the skin temperature cooled down, the better.

keep the animal's head out in the open, and have someone else pour the cold water right on the cloth (Figure 34).

If you miss the moment the cat is burned, you may not know it's been burned until hours or even a day later. Signs will be fidgeting, a distinct sensitivity and redness to the skin, and perhaps some loss of hair. Use a towel to restrain the animal as shown in Figure 34, but don't cover the burned area. Very gently clean the area with cool water and mild soap, then clip the hair from around the burn. Apply an over-the-counter first aid cream containing an antibiotic. Lacking that, use plain petroleum jelly. *Do not* use butter, cooking oils, or lard.

If, after you've treated the burn, the cat seems reasonably content, and you can't get to a veterinarian for some reason, keep the burned area clean. You should also cover it with a clean, lint-free cloth and confine the cat to protect the injury. A first- or second-degree burn affecting a significant area of the animal's body, however, will require veterinary attention in the *very near future.*

Heat Burns, Third-Degree. There will be obvious and severe damage to skin and underlying tissue. There may be deeper internal damage, particularly if the burn has been caused by flames, and if much smoke has been inhaled. All sensation will be lost in the burned area, and the animal will likely be semiconscious. This will make administering immediate, but gentle, first aid considerably easier than for a conscious cat.

Do not flush the wound with cold water. Apply a cold, wet towel or T-shirt to the burn. Keeping the animal as quiet as possible will lessen pain, but be alert for signs of shock. If they are present, treat them, then keep the burn covered with the wet cloth while you get to a veterinarian as fast as you can.

What if you can't get to a veterinarian because your car won't start or you're stuck for transportation?

Keep the burn covered. Keep the dressing wet with a solution of 1 teaspoon salt to a quart of water. Change the dressing frequently. If the cat is able to swallow on its own, the delay in getting medical help means it must have fluid therapy to prevent dehydration. The solution you'll need to administer consists of 1 teaspoon salt and 1 teaspoon baking soda in a quart of water. Figures 35A and 35B show how to give your cat fluids.

There's no gentle way to conclude this section on third-degree heat burns. You won't like what is recommended and will find

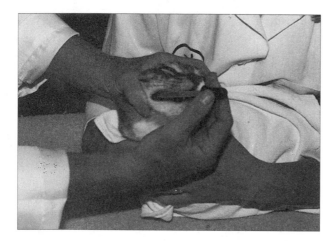

Figures 35A, 35B. Restrain cat by wrapping body and legs in a towel or blanket. Fluids can be administered by using an eyedropper (A) or paper cup (B), as long as they're poured into the side of the animal's mouth as shown.

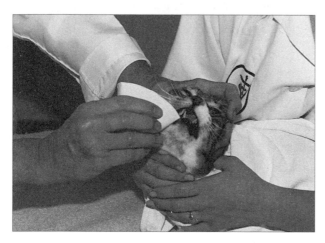

doing it very, very difficult. Nevertheless, if your cat suffers a third-degree burn exceeding 10 to 15 percent of its body area, it is extremely doubtful that it will recover and be able to live a normal life. Be prepared. If your veterinarian advises you to do so, allow your badly burned cat to be put to sleep.

Chemical Burns, In General. If you keep cleaning agents, paint thinners, and other harsh, household chemicals behind closed doors, your cat can't get hurt by them. If you're using such chemicals, and your cat is nearby, get the cat out of the area. A firm "Scat!" will injure your pet far less than the drain cleaner you're about to pour into a stopped-up sink.

Various kinds of household products are the biggest offenders when it comes to feline chemical burns. The gasoline and kerosene stored in your garage run a close second. Coming in third are mace and a wide variety of other chemical irritants people throw at felines out of viciousness and annoyance. Mostly viciousness.

Before we begin to describe treatment of specific types of chemical burns, there are certain procedures with which you should become familar. You are advised to use the first, demonstrated in Figures 36A and 36B below, if the chemical has spilled, or been thrown, into a cat's eyes.

Figures 36A, 36B.
Restrain the cat with a
full body / leg wrap and
have someone immobilize
the animal's head (A).
Use an eyedropper or
sponge to flush eye with
clean water (B).

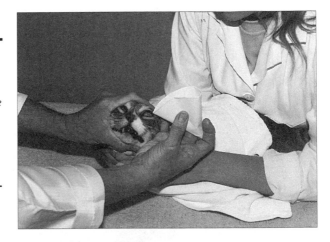

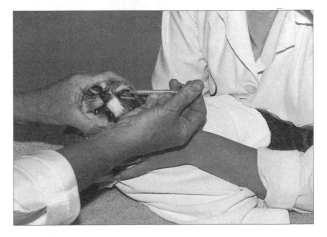

The second (Figure 37) or third (Figure 38) procedures, along with confinement, should be applied when there is a need to prevent the cat from biting or scratching at the chemically burned area. Be assured, it will if it can, and by doing so the cat will only make matters worse.

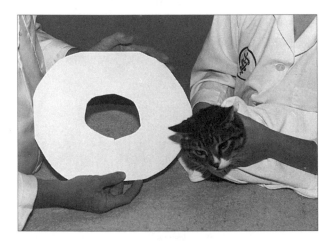

Figures 37A, 37B. Cut a circular piece of cardboard half again as large as the diameter of the animal's body, then cut a hole large enough to fit around the cat's neck (A). Slit the collar and fit it over the head and around the neck (B). Tape up the slit to secure the collar in place.

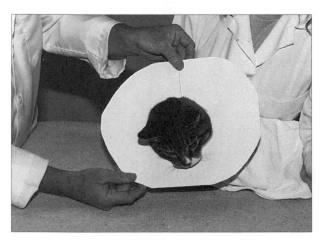

Please note that all of the treatments described assume that you are either on the scene at the time the accident happens or on the scene very soon afterwards.

Chemical Burns of the Body (Acidic). Vinegar is acid; some photographic chemicals are acid. If you know that whatever caused the burn

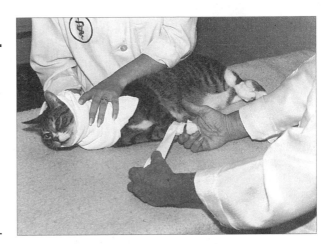

Figure 38. With an assistant restraining the cat's head as shown, tape the front feet together (and the hind feet if necessary, depending on the area involved). It will prevent further damage to the injured area on the trip to a veterinarian.

contained acid, mix 1 teaspoon baking soda with 1 quart water. Flush the affected area very, very generously with this solution. It neutralizes the acid, so pour it on. The affected skin will be inflamed and sensitive. After the flooding, apply an antibiotic first aid cream.

Chemical Burns to the Eyes (Acidic). Using the technique for head restraint previously demonstrated, wash out the eyes with a solution of 1 teaspoon baking soda to 1 quart of water. After washing, you may apply a drop of mineral oil or olive oil to either or both eyes to soothe and protect them.

Chemical Burns to the Body (Alkaline). Most household cleaning products are alkaline, and bleach is probably the most common example. To treat an alkaline burn, use plain water. Lots and lots of plain water. When the area has been thoroughly flushed clean, apply an antibiotic first aid cream.

Chemical Burns to the Eyes (Alkaline). Flush the eyes with clean, cool water and use a drop or two of mineral or olive oil to soothe them.

Chemical Burns (Petroleum Products or Turpentine). We're covering these separately for a good reason. Such burns are initially superficial, though very painful. The real danger is that petroleum products and turpentine can be absorbed into the skin and eventually cause systemic complications. Those complications can become critical and may include pulmonary edema (fluid in the lungs).

If the body is affected, flush the burned area with plenty of water. After flushing, soak it with mineral oil and gently rub the oil into the skin. Let the mineral oil do its work for a few minutes, then wash it off with lukewarm water and mild soap or shampoo. If the eyes are affected, flush them with water and apply drops of mineral or olive oil.

NOTE: With any petroleum product or turpentine burn, see your veterinarian as soon as possible for an evaluation of secondary problems.

Chemical Burns (Feet). If the chemical causing the burn is *acidic,* treat the injured paw or paws as you would an acidic burn to the body as described above. If the chemical is *alkaline,* follow the given treatment outlined for such burns. In either case, the animal's paws will require protective bandages. (See Figures 39A and 39B). For *petroleum product or turpentine* burns, treat as you would a similar burn to the body. DO NOT bandage. Transport the cat to your veterinarian for further examination.

Frostbite. Extreme cold affects the skin in ways similar to extreme heat. Circulation is compromised, the skin becomes irritated, but, unlike a heat burn, the signs of frostbite are subtle. It isn't accompanied by a piercing cry of pain and anger. You may not become aware the cat has been "bitten" until later, when the tips of its ears or the pads on its feet begin to peel. At such time, apply plain petroleum jelly to the area to assist in healing the damage already done.

If, however, the cat comes in from the cold and you observe the following signs, you can treat the frostbite and, hopefully, lessen its effects. Does the cat walk about in a tender-footed manner? Does it shake its head with great frequency? Does it continuously fuss with its ears or some other part of its body? If any or all of these symptoms are evident, apply mild heat to the affected area. A blow dryer set on low temperature is an excellent tool for the task. Lacking one, you can apply a warm, wet cloth instead. Not hot, *warm.* Once the cat appears to be more comfortable, dip a

Figures 39A, 39B.
Gently extend the foot,
apply bandage over burn
(A), and wrap with gauze
to secure the bandage in
place (B).

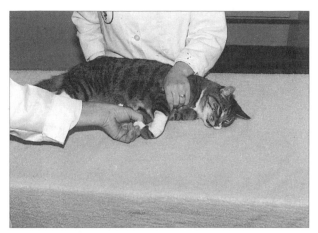

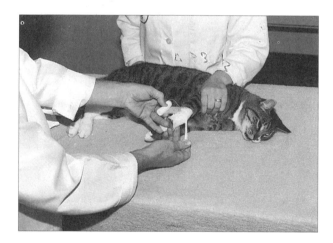

fingertip or two into plain petroleum jelly and gently massage ears, feet, or whatever has been frostbitten to stimulate circulation.

Electric Burns. Every Christmas, a large number of cats of all ages suffer electric burns to the mouth. In most cases, those burns originate on or in the immediate vicinity of a brightly decorated Christmas tree. Cats find them almost irresistible until they get burned by chewing through the cord of a string of lights. They only do it once, though. Cats are entirely too intelligent to make the same mistake twice.

An electric burn of the mouth can be either first-, second-, or third-degree. Since the mouth itself has been burned, treating it will be difficult. You may be able to flush it with cold water and apply a cold compress. If the animal is amenable, do it, and get to a veterinarian quickly. If the cat won't allow you to wash out its mouth, you still have to get medical help—and just as quickly.

Electric burns burn deep. With no pun intended, they often cause shock, as well as respiratory problems and other serious systemic damage. For those reasons, the best first aid treatment for an electric burn is taking the fastest route to the doctor's office.

3

PREVENTABLE
CAT-TASTROPHES

We could refer to the subjects covered in this chapter as nontraumatic accidents, but, in consideration of your emotions as a cat lover, we'll just call them *less* traumatic. In these cases, there are no gaping wounds, no broken bones, no cars or other moving objects involved. The injuries and conditions do not usually create an emergency, and may even lend themselves to home care, but they do require immediate attention.

Each and every problem that follows not only could, but definitely will, develop into an emergency of the worst kind if it goes undetected or ignored. Don't misunderstand. There is no intention here of transforming you, the cat owner, into a diagnostician. Diagnosis is for doctors and you should never — never — attempt to practice it. On the other hand, there *is* every intention in this chapter of encouraging you to practice first aid in its most basic form: preventive medicine.

GENERAL SKIN PROBLEMS

Skin problems are a primary concern with all cats. The prevention of them is mostly a matter of diet and grooming. A balanced diet is essential if a good coat is to be maintained. Fortunately, most commercial cat foods today can successfully provide a proper diet— at least they can for the average cat. What do we mean by an "average cat"? A cat not susceptible to skin problems caused by allergic reactions. A common allergenic culprit is a food that most cats love: fish. Don't panic. If your cat has been filling up on fish-based food with no ill effects, you probably own one of those average cats we spoke of, but diets high in fish can and do cause allergy-related skin problems. As a matter of fact, cats can be allergic to many of the same things that plague humans. Before we go on to specifics, please bear in mind that, if your cat has a skin problem and it doesn't respond to home care in two or three days, seek professional medical help.

Miliary Dermatitis. It's a common problem, and its cause can be diet, dirt, fleas, pollen, or a number of other irritating things too numerous to mention.

Regardless of the cause, the manifestation on the cat can usually be felt as little scabs around the neck and head. The scabs come from small, inflamed areas, and the disease will progress along the lower back and around the tail. There will be partial loss of hair, and your cat will be very unhappy while it scratches itself raw.

Omit fish from the cat's diet, though it may not be the cause. Even if the food container doesn't say "tuna," or "salmon," it could contain fish oil or fish meal as a base. Maintain cleanliness with good grooming and bathing, but check with your veterinarian on what to use to bathe the cat. The problem could also be fleas, so read the section (pages 77-79) on fleas.

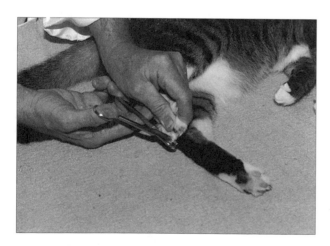

Figure 40. Use only *scissor-type clippers available at your pet supply store or through your veterinarian. Place your forefinger on top of the nail and use your thumb to apply pressure to the pad of the foot; doing so extends the nail to be cut. Clip just in* front *of the pink portion of the nail to avoid severe bleeding.*

If the cat has a raw, red area that it's only making worse by scratching, apply an over-the-counter antibiotic cream to the area and cover it with a gauze bandage, as was shown in Figures 18A and 18B on page 37. To insure further protection to the area you've just treated and to prevent the cat from disturbing your handiwork, fit it with an Elizabethan collar (see Figure 37, page 66), cut its nails (Figure 40), or do both.

Feline Acne. In cats, as in people, acne is an infection of the hair follicles. It will show up around and under your cat's chin as blackheads and pustules. The cat may give you a clue it's afflicted by rubbing its chin on the rug or worrying it with its paws. The chin itself may appear to be swollen.

Reach for the hydrogen-peroxide-based teenage acne medicine at your drugstore. Apply it once or twice daily. Positive results should be evident in about forty-eight hours. If not, your cat's acne will require the attention of a veterinarian and the application of prescribed antibiotics.

Ringworm. This fungal infection shows up as little, irritated areas with mild scabbing around the head and paws. If it is infecting other parts of the body, there may be some loss of hair. That's the good news.

The bad news is, if you don't get your cat to a veterinarian, your whole family can become infested. Ringworm is highly contagious, especially among young animals, and not at all particular whether the young animal is feline or *Homo sapiens*. You can cut down on the infection with iodine-based shampoos, but be careful of your cat's eyes when shampooing, and know that all the shampoo in the world may not cure ringworm. The only cure for your cat is oral or topical antifungal drugs, prescribed and administered by a veterinarian.

Abscesses. We don't mean to scold, but poor feline health care and abscesses keep pretty close company. Almost anything can cause an abscess: an animal bite or a retained foreign body, for example. The list goes on, and regular visits to a veterinarian may eliminate the possibility of your ever having to do what follows.

If your cat has an abscess, it is open and draining, and there's

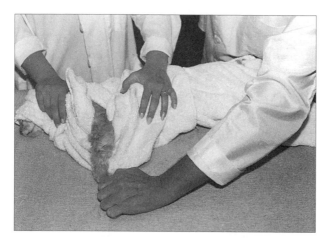

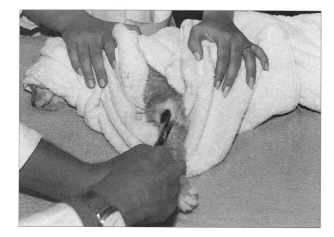

Figures 41A, 41B, 41C. Using a towel or small blanket, restrain the animal and leave only the area to be worked on exposed (A). Clip hair (B) and cleanse area around the wound with soap and water or peroxide. Expand the wound with scissors or forceps. Swab wound with a cotton-tipped swab dipped in peroxide (C). Continue to keep wound open by swabbing it the same way on a daily basis, using first aid cream instead of peroxide. Remember, the idea is to let the injury heal from the inside out.

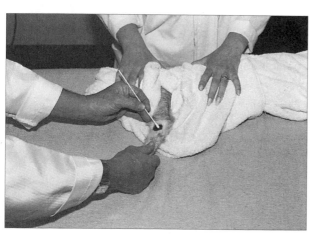

no medical help in sight, restrain the cat and clip the area around the wound (Figures 41A-41C). Flush gently with warm water to remove surface dirt and any residue from the clipped area. Your next task is to keep the wound open, reduce the infection, and encourage healing from the inside out. The latter is most important. If the wound heals over before the infection has exhausted itself, all you've done is create another habitat for another abscess.

SKIN PARASITES

There are the obvious ones, with which you're no doubt familiar, and some downright disgusting ones you've probably never heard of before. Disgusting and dangerous. We'll begin, however, with the most obvious of all.

The Flea. The flea is the parasite that has been with us the longest. It will most likely, and unfortunately, plague us forever. Let's face it, the flea is a survivor, and it multiplies prodigiously. It doesn't care whether the weather is hot, cold, damp, soaking wet, or fossil dry. It lives for days, even weeks, without food or drink, and does its damage while spending less than 10 percent of its time on an animal. During its brief visitations, the flea doesn't just cause skin problems. It can also carry diseases, and it is the host for tapeworm eggs. A cat bitten by a host flea will naturally bite back, swallow the flea, and often develop a tapeworm.

Getting rid of fleas takes more than a casual approach. Treating an already infested cat, and then believing that you are permanently free of fleas, is like putting a piece of adhesive tape on the San Andreas fault. Total freedom from this hardiest of pests begins at your local garden center. Request a spray pesticide known to be effective against fleas and harmless to cats. If there's any doubt—even the slightest—which pesticide meets both criteria, ask your veterinarian before applying a drop of it. Also be sure to check the label and follow all of the manufacturer's precautions for use. Once assured, spray the lawn and garden freely and as often as the instructions on the bottle or container direct. So much for the outdoor breeding grounds of Mr. Flea.

But suppose the fleas have taken up residence in your house?

If they have, chances are very good that the cat won't be the only one scratching. Though many commonly sold household sprays and bombs will kill fleas, check with your veterinarian to see which offers the best combination of effectiveness and safety. And don't, for heaven's sake, spray them directly on your cat. As an alternative to bombs and sprays, light up a sulfur candle or two, close up the house, and take a nice, all-day trip. Sulfur candles stink mightily, but they also work. If the infestation is severe, and all of the above fails, you will have to call in a professional exterminator.

As for ridding the cat of fleas, there are many over-the-counter preparations to be had. But be forewarned: Before using anything, make sure the product label states that it's safe to use on cats, then make sure that it's safe to use on *your* cat. Some shampoos and sprays that are harmless to older cats are far from harmless to young ones.

Reoccurrence of fleas on your cat, assuming you've treated the cat's environment as described above, can be controlled by periodic shampooing and the application of a flea spray. Only products that can be used frequently and safely should be employed, particularly the sprays. Some have a residual effect which can be cumulative and to which your cat may have an adverse reaction. Flea powders, though effective, can and do accumulate on the animal's hair. The cat, in the process of grooming itself, will ingest the residual powder and may experience a systemic reaction.

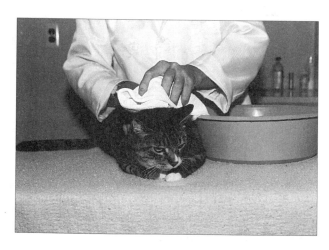

Figure 42. Most cats highly resent being placed directly into water, so don't do it. Place the animal next to a sink or basin and use a sponge or washcloth to bathe and rinse **thoroughly.**

Our recommendation for controlling fleas on your cat calls for grooming and shampooing. Grooming two or three times a week will actually comb out the pests, but don't shake the comb out onto a rug. Shake it into an insecticide solution. Shampooing should take place once every two or three weeks. No sudden plunges into tub or basin, please, and *please* trim your cat's nails before giving it a shampoo. Place a bucket containing whatever sudsy mix you're using *beside* the animal and sponge-bathe it (Figure 42).

Head Mites. Appropriately named, these microscopic creatures shun all other parts of the body. They cause intense itching, equally intense scratching, loss of hair, and severe skin irritation. A veterinarian's diagnosis is required to confirm the presence of head mites, but if your cat is attacking its face and head with frequency and suffering the symptoms just described, you can provide temporary relief by applying an over-the-counter antibiotic and cortisone ointment. Notice we said *temporary.* Any permanent solution will only result from a trip to the doctor's office.

Body/Mange Mites. Also microscopic, the female of this species actually burrows a little tunnel under the skin to lay her eggs. Though not as common in cats as in dogs, the result of this homemaking action is the same: inflammation, itching, and loss of hair. However, what kills mange mites on dogs can't always be used safely on cats. Discomfort can be temporarily relieved with an antibiotic and cortisone ointment, but you have to get a positive diagnosis and a recommendation for further treatment from your veterinarian.

Lice. Smaller than fleas and bigger than mites, lice live on the skin's surface, are bluish white, and can been seen with a magnifying glass. They are transmitted from one animal to another by close contact, and are not that common in house cats. Lice cause a lot of scratching and dandruff, and they can be readily eliminated with a reliable flea shampoo.

Ticks. We don't know why, specifically, but ticks aren't as much of a problem with cats as they are with dogs. It may be the nature of the animal's hair, which doesn't allow the invader to get a good grip, or it may simply be part of feline nature, or intelligence, to avoid ticks. Whatever the reason, the average household cat doesn't pick them up. Let's suppose, though, that your cat decides not to be average, and you feel a small lump while petting your cat that turns out to be a tick. Ticks carry diseases and should be removed (Figure 43). They should be removed very carefully, for some of the diseases they carry are as bad for your health as your cat's. Maybe worse.

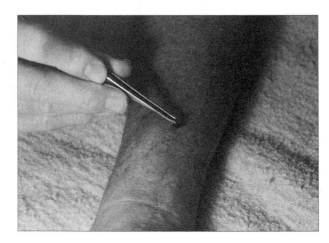

Figure 43. Don't use your fingers to remove ticks. Ticks may carry Lyme or other diseases. Grasp the tick as close to the skin as possible with a pair of tweezers. Employ a steady but gentle pull up and toward the tick's head to remove the pest. Then clean the bitten area with peroxide.

The Warble. We promised you some disgusting skin parasites, and this is one of them. It can also be deadly. Warbles are the larval stage of the Cutareba fly. The Cutareba lays its egg on a cow, the egg hatches, and the larva chews a hole in the cow's skin. It then penetrates beneath the skin, forms a sac, and develops to pupal stage. The hole bored to make entry serves both as an air vent for the pupa and a route out for the fly that the pupa becomes. The hole never closes, not even when the cow becomes cowhide.

What does a cow with a hole in its skin have to do with your cat? Another version of the Cutareba, sort of a first cousin, seems to prefer cats to cows—particularly kittens and older, sick cats.

Warbles can be fatal if there are more than one or two present by creating secondary infections and placing undue stresses on the host animal's system. They are not easily seen. You may feel them first as a small swelling accompanied by a discharge. Look closer for a small hole in the skin. Look even closer with a magnifying glass and you will see the pupa moving around under the hole.

Do not squeeze the area in an attempt to force the pupa out. The animal's immune system has built up a sac around the warble. Squeezing could rupture the sac and cause an acute allergic reaction or even *death*.

A warble must be removed intact surgically, with a local anesthesia. The sooner the better. Once it has been removed, your task will be to encourage healing and prevent infection as you would with a puncture wound or abscess, as shown in Figure 44.

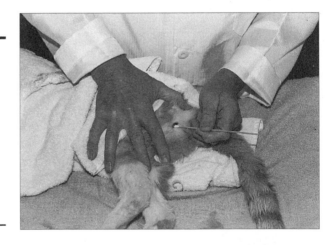

Figure 44. After you have clipped the wound, cleaned it, and enlarged it with forceps, use a cotton-tipped swab coated with first aid cream or petroleum jelly on a daily basis to keep the wound open and encourage healing from the inside out.

Maggots. Whether they are more revolting than warbles, we leave up to you. Assuredly, they are every bit as serious and far more common.

Like the warble, maggots prefer kittens or debilitated older cats. They are the larval stage of the common housefly, which find soiled areas of the body or untreated abscesses an attractive place to lay its eggs. The eggs hatch and become active maggots. Unlike the warble, maggots are easily seen. They look like little garden grubs. Maggots don't make a home of the holes they drill in the skin; they do worse. They keep burrowing, eating, and producing toxic waste from their digestive excretions. They are capable of entering the eyes, mouth, nose, and rectum. They are also capable of gnawing their way from body surface to body interior.

While the maggots go about their nasty business, the animal reacts as it would to a foreign body: Its system tries to fight off the intruders. The longer the battle goes on, the weaker the animal grows. If for some reason you don't see the maggots or don't notice your cat's increasingly weakened condition, you can smell the trouble. It will remind you of meat that has gone bad.

Our first aid recommendations only apply if circumstances prevent you from securing immediate veterinary help. They are surface measures and will not correct or prevent deeper damage. Wash the affected area with mild soap and water. Flush it, then flush it again with fresh solution. Use tweezers to remove those maggots that are burrowing — you may have to clip the cat's hair to do this. Don't use an insecticide, but do use a soothing first aid cream. Watch your cat closely for twenty-four to forty-eight hours. If new hatchlings appear, tweeze them off, then repeat the washing process. At any rate, get your cat to a veterinarian as soon as possible.

Maggots are easily avoided. Don't leave a kitten or older cat outside on a warm summer day. If your cat has been outside on such a day, examine it when it comes indoors. If eggs have been laid, they will appear on the hair as a white, pasty substance that can be washed or clipped off before hatching occurs.

CLAWS AND NAILS

Preventing problems, including the problem of you or a family member getting painfully scratched, calls for frequent trimming. Cats don't wear their nails down like dogs do. They'll sharpen them on a clawing post or piece of furniture, but that only serves to shed the outer shell. Your cat won't like having its claws trimmed, but with proper restraint you can do it yourself (Figure 45). If you can't, your veterinarian will have to do it for you.

Ingrown Claws. If you can hear your cat walking, this is what's making the clicking noise. A claw, or claws, has grown in a circle and right back into the footpad. The animal will be limping and, if the ingrown condition is severe, there may be bleeding around

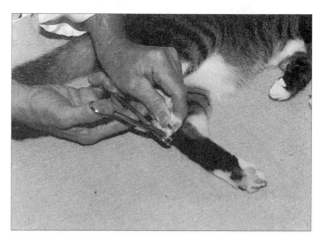

*Figure 45. Use **only** scissor-type clippers available at your pet supply store or through your veterinarian. Place your forefinger on top of the nail and use your thumb to apply pressure to the pad of the foot; doing so extends the nail to be cut. Clip just **in front** of the pink portion of the nail to avoid severe bleeding.*

the feet. An ingrown claw must be clipped and the penetrating end removed from the foot. If it isn't, it can create all the complications any foreign body causes, including serious infection.

Use the method of restraint and the curved clippers shown above. If, after clipping, the imbedded nail doesn't fall out on its own, it can be easily removed with a pair of tweezers. Treat the injured pad like a puncture wound by washing it with soap and water and applying hydrogen peroxide. Don't panic if the pad bleeds — it's common — and don't bandage the wound. Confine the cat in a box or carrier, apply petroleum jelly to the injury daily, and keep a sharp eye out for signs of infection.

Broken Nails. If your cat is a homebody, you probably won't have to concern yourself with such things. If your cat is the outdoor type, however, fighting, climbing trees, and making fast getaways will eventually result in a shredded or split nail. Usually, the dew claw — the one up the paw a little — is the one most frequently injured. The injury is followed by limping, licking, and, quite often, bleeding. If left untreated, it will constantly be catching on things, becoming progressively more irritated and more of a problem.

Damaged nails are very sensitive. You can be certain your cat won't want you to touch them and will have no intention of cooperating with you. Restraint, as shown in Figure 46, is

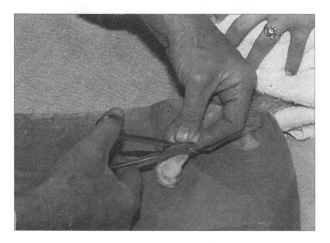

Figure 46. Have a helper restrain the entire cat except for the leg and nail involved. Quickly trim the nail back to normal length following the cutting procedure for clipping nails demonstrated in Figure 45 (page 83). Remember not to cut back into the nail's pink area, which could create severe bleeding. After trimming the nail (shown here is the dew claw) back, clip matted hair if necessary, then cleanse the area with mild soap and water or peroxide. A bandage may be needed.

necessary, as are proper, curved clippers and some fast action on your part to minimize discomfort—both yours and your cat's. After clipping, wash the area with plain, mild soap and water or hydrogen peroxide.

ORAL PROBLEMS

No matter what the problem, the indications that your cat has something wrong with its mouth are pretty much the same. They include difficulty in chewing; lack of interest in food; obvious pawing or scratching at the mouth; a strong, foul breath; and bleeding from the gums. You can only resolve some of the problems some of the time.

Tartar. Initially the most common and least serious of oral problems, tartar builds up in cats' mouths for the same reason it builds up in people's mouths. The fact that cats prefer soft foods doesn't help, because soft food promotes that buildup. Diet can't totally control tartar, though, because cats don't chew with their gums and that's where tartar first takes hold. Cat toothbrushes and cat toothpastes are available and can be used as shown in Figure 47 to prevent or control buildup. If you notice tartar on your cat's teeth, you can also scrape it off with your thumbnail, as shown below. Not shown is the trip to the veterinarian you'll be taking if the buildup is beyond your ability, or your cat's willingness, to remove it.

Gingivitis. This doesn't happen overnight. It can be the result of poor dental hygiene, infections, or some other health problem. Whatever the cause, tartar has built up to the point where the

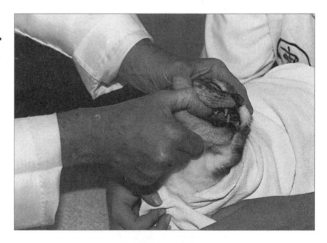

Figures 47A, 47B. Using full body restraint, plus assistance to keep the cat's head still, place one hand on top of the animal's head with thumb positioned in corner of jaw to force mouth open and hold it open (A). Use thumbnail of free hand or a stiff-bristled toothbrush to attack tartar (B).

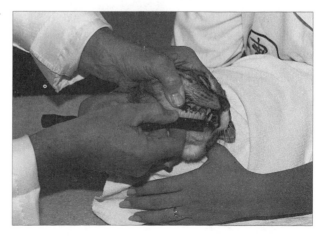

gums are extremely inflamed, and there is bleeding, bad breath, and drooling.

Temporary relief can be achieved by flushing the animal's mouth with a salt water solution: about 1 teaspoon in a small glass of water used on a gauze pad, sponge, or in a paper cup (Figure 48). Don't consider this a cure for gingivitis. Left medically untended the condition will worsen into periodontal disease, and the teeth will loosen and fall out. In older cats, periodontitis can result in oral tumors: small, hard, pea- or bean-sized growths on the gums that must be surgically removed. Malignant tumors can also occur, in which case far more drastic surgery is required.

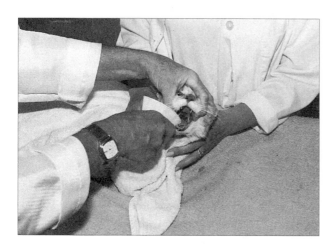

Figure 48. With full body restraint, and assistance to immobilize the cat's head, use a saturated gauze pad, sponge, or paper cup to apply salt water solution to the gums. The solution is prepared by dissolving 1 teaspoon of salt in a 6-ounce glass of water.

Foreign Bodies—Oral (General). Curiosity may not always kill the cat, but it sure will cause it to pick up things and carry them off. Bones and sticks are the most common, and just as commonly end up wedged across the roof of the mouth. Among the signs that precisely such a thing has happened are futile pawing or scratching by the cat in attempts to remove whatever is stuck in there, difficulty in chewing its food, and an odor you can't miss if the foreign object has been present for any length of time.

Figures 49A and 49B show how to take a look in the mouth and use needle-nosed pliers to remove the object. You'll have to do it quickly, though.

Sometimes, a small sliver or two of bone can become caught

between a cat's teeth. Gums will be inflamed, and there may be a bit of bleeding. Using the restraint procedure demonstrated in Figures 49A and 49B, you may be able to dislodge the bit(s) of bone with a fingernail. If they don't come out easily (and, more often than not, they won't) a veterinarian will have to do it for you using dental picks.

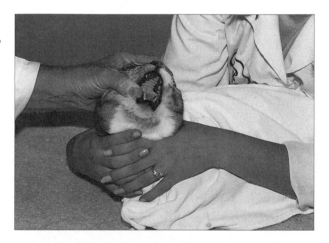

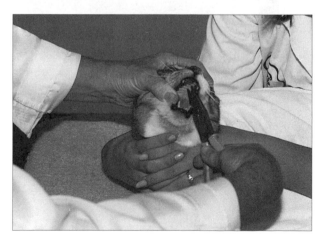

Figures 49A, 49B. Full body restraint and help in holding the cat's head absolutely still are required. Place one hand on top of cat's head; use that hand's thumb in the corner of the jaws to force the mouth open (A). With needle-nosed pliers, firmly grasp the foreign body and quickly remove it (B). If the foreign body is a fish hook, make no attempt to remove it; put the animal in a box and get to your veterinarian.

Foreign Body — Oral (Fish Hook). It's not the rod in the hands of the fisherman that catches the cat, it's the rod just returned home, smelling fishy and perhaps with a bit of bait left on the hook.

Never, never try to remove a fish hook. Not from the mouth; not from anywhere on your cat for that matter. Cut the line off 3 or 4 inches from the hook and transport the animal to a veterinarian immediately.

Foreign Body — Oral (String). More often than not you won't be aware of it. If you can see it, *don't pull on it.* You don't know where the other end is. Confine the cat and take it to your veterinarian.

Foreign Body — Throat. Usually, a piece of bone or stick is the culprit and will get lodged just beyond the downward curve of the tongue. Much choking and gagging accompanied by severe stress will make restraining your cat all but impossible. If the animal is cooperative, however, you may be able to hold it still long enough to open its mouth and see if the foreign body is visible. If you can see the bit of bone or stick, quickly grasp it with a pair of forceps or needle-nosed pliers and pull gently (Figure 50). If it comes out, fine. If it doesn't, don't try and muscle it out even if your cat is willing to give you a second chance. Transport the animal to your veterinarian immediately.

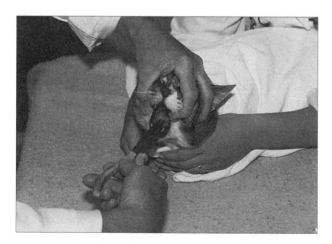

*Figure 50. This is another case where full body restraint and help in restraining the cat's head is vital. Once that's accomplished, and **only** if you can see the foreign body isn't a fish hook, grasp the upper jaw with your free hand and use forceps or needle-nosed pliers to grasp and quickly remove it.*

If you can't see the foreign body, and you're sure it's not a fishhook, you may be able to dislodge it with a feline version of the Heimlich maneuver, as shown in Figures 51A and 51B.

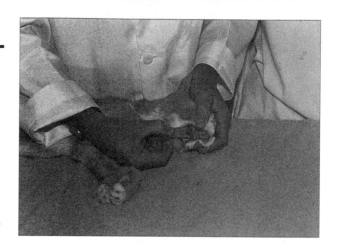

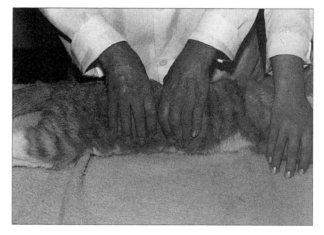

Figures 51A, 51B. Maintain an open airway by keeping head extended and tongue pulled out to the side of the mouth (A). Place both your hands on the cat's rib cage toward the rear (B). Push down sharply and release quickly. Repeat until foreign body is dislodged or animal is breathing normally. If, after repeated attempts, you are unsuccessful, transport the cat to a veterinarian immediately.

VOMITING AND DIARRHEA

Too much of something that tastes good to your cat, but that isn't very good for its digestive system, causes vomiting and/or diarrhea. So does eating something that shouldn't have been eaten in the first place; also,infectious diseases, bacterial infections, any one of many viral infections, and foreign bodies that get swallowed.

Vomiting. All you can do is soothe things on an overnight basis until you can reach a veterinarian. Take all food and water away and attempt to administer an over-the-counter stomach coating agent using an eyedropper or paper cup as shown in Figures 35A and 35B on page 64.

Diarrhea. If the cat is having very loose stools, but isn't throwing up, appears bright, and has an interest in taking food and water, you have a couple of choices of things to feed it. Boiled, lean hamburger and boiled rice mixed together is one. Strained baby food — beef, lamb, or chicken — is the other. In addition, a teaspoon of stomach coating medicine administered on the hour will help settle things down. However, if your cat doesn't respond to treatment after two or three days, consult your veterinarian.

INTERNAL PARASITES

There are some truly bizarre parasites in the world of cats. We are limiting this discussion to those parasites most often found in the American house cat. They're bad enough. The most common among them are congenital, having been passed from queen to kitten, and they present a serious problem to the system of a growing cat by placing a greater demand on it. A heavy infestation of congenital parasites can be extremely troublesome and even fatal. We underscore the seriousness of such infestations in the hope that owners of kittens will have their pets, and their pet's stool, examined by a veterinarian very early in life and diligently follow any regimen of parasite treatment the doctor may recommend.

Roundworm. Official name, ascarid. Round in shape, they are quite frequently found in kittens. How did they get there? The eggs of the roundworm are passed in the stool of an adult cat, picked up by another adult via a shared litter pan or during a grass-eating expedition in the yard, and develops into larvae within the second cat, which travel through the system and become encased in the new host's body. If the host is female and becomes pregnant, the larvae become active and migrate into the unborn kitten's body. After birth, the larvae continue their migration through the lungs and up the windpipe. At that point the kitten will either spit up the unwelcome travellers or swallow them, in which case a mature worm will develop in the intestine.

Early signs of roundworm in kittens include coughing, gagging, and difficulty in breathing due to the migration of the larvae.

Later signs are those of what we call an "unthrifty" cat. The larvae have matured into intestinal worms, which compete with the animal for nourishment, cause blockages, and inhibit proper digestion. As a result, the cat looks poorly, doesn't have a good coat, and shows a distinct potbelly.

Diagnosis at this later stage is by veterinary analysis of the animal's stool. If eggs are present, medication will be administered which will cause the mature roundworms — about the same size as the diameter of a small lead pencil — to be passed out during the course of a normal bowel movement. If detected and treated early on, roundworm infestation is not overly serious. If ignored, it can be fatal.

A final word about these parasites. Roundworm eggs can be passed from cats to children. The eggs will develop into larvae which will migrate through the child's system as they do in a kitten's, though they will not mature into adult worms. Therefore, keep the kids away from the litter box and the cat away from the kid's sandbox. Remember, roundworm is transmitted by coming in direct contact with the pet's contaminated stool.

Hookworm. Common in both young and adult cats, hookworm is acquired the same way as roundworm, but hookworm eggs will hatch in stool-contaminated soil. The larvae can and will penetrate intact skin, then go through the same life cycle as roundworm larvae in your cat's body. Because hookworm larvae are almost microscopic, however, they don't cause the pulmonary problems the much larger roundworm larvae do. The prevention of hookworm calls for daily cleaning of the litter box, good general hygiene, and equally good policing of any outdoor areas frequented by your cat.

As adults, hookworms attach themselves to the intestinal wall and feed on the animal's blood. This parasitic form of vampirism can destroy a young cat in short order by making it critically anemic. Symptoms that hookworms are at work include weakness in the animal, poor appetite, bloody diarrhea, and pale gum and inner lip membranes.

Because hookworm can be so devastating to young cats, stool analysis by your veterinarian is recommended at three to four weeks of age. And, because it can be fatal to any cat, appearance of the symptoms described above should soon be followed by a medical diagnosis and the *prescription* of medication corresponding to your cat's condition. Avoid over-the-counter cures.

Whipworm. Once again, the parasite is transmitted via stool and contaminated soil. The larvae do not migrate through the body as roundworm larvae do and cannot be transmitted to the unborn. In small numbers, whipworm is of little consequence. In larger numbers, it favors the lower bowel, causing inflammation and intermittent diarrhea. Though annoying, whipworm is not life-threatening in an otherwise healthy kitten or cat, but, if the animal is debilitated for other reasons, it can be the final straw.

Anytime your cat experiences chronic diarrhea, seek a veterinary diagnosis. It may be caused by whipworm or hookworm.

Tapeworm. Though perhaps the most common parasite found in adult cats, tapeworm is not passed directly from cat to cat. It requires an intermediate host. Among the creatures capable of serving the tapeworm's need, the most ready, willing, and able is the flea. We'll explain how something so small can play host to something several hundred times its size.

A cat, once infested, harbors the tapeworm, which produces segments. The worm sheds these segments periodically and the sheddings can be seen around the affected animal's backside or in its bedding. They are about the size of a grain of rice, and they are alive. These segments don't live long, but they contain eggs, which in turn are shed when the segment dies. A flea feeding on the debris existing on the affected cat's body will pick up the egg and digest it. The egg develops within the flea. The next step in the development of a tapeworm is that a noninfested cat gets close enough to the infested cat for the egg-carrying flea to relocate. Flea bites cat, cat bites flea, swallows it, and thereby acquires a tapeworm of its very own.

Tapeworms don't produce a great degree of debilitation in an otherwise healthy animal. Actually, a cat can tolerate a number of tapeworms and still manage very well, but if your cat has them you'll obviously want it to be rid of them — tapeworms do rob it of nutrients. And, as the cat grows older, the loss of those nutrients

We'd love your thoughts...

Your reactions, criticisms, things you did or didn't like about this Storey/Garden Way Publishing Book. Please use space below (or write a letter if you'd prefer — even send photos!) telling how you've made use of the information...how you've put it to work...the more details the better! Thanks in advance for your help in building our library of good Storey/Garden Way Publishing books.

M John Story
Publisher

Book Title: _____

Purchased From: _____

Comments: _____

_____

_____

_____

_____

_____

_____

Your Name: _____

Address: _____

☐ Please check here if you'd like our latest Storey/Garden Way Publishing Books for Country Living Catalog.

☐ You have my permission to quote from my comments, and use these quotations in ads, brochures, mail, and other promotions used to market your books.

Signed _____ Date _____

will unfortunately manifest itself in one way or another.

To prevent tapeworm you have to control the flea population. Reread what has already been advised on ridding your cat of fleas (pages 77-79). To rid your cat of tapeworm, do not use an over-the-counter worm medicine. See your veterinarian, who will prescribe medication befitting the animal's age and condition.

Coccidia. These are not worms, but belong to a family of microscopic organisms called protozoa, and they occur due to poor hygiene. The organism, shed in an affected cat's stool, is not immediately infectious. It incubates in the excrement until it becomes vile, and is so small it can be inhaled in the dust particles raised from a litter box. As the protozoa travel through the body they generally don't cause systemic infections, but they can, and the effect on the lungs and central nervous system will result in a very sick animal. In most cases, the protozoa settle in the intestinal tract, causing irritation, mucousy diarrhea, or diarrhea with blood. In very young kittens, a serious invasion can lead to severe dehydration and very possibly death.

Coccidia can be controlled with antibiotics (the prescription of which requires proper veterinary diagnosis), and are sometimes treated with fluid therapy. The best way to prevent coccidia is to know the birthplace or origin of your kitten or cat, have it examined, and follow all the rules for hygiene we've already outlined.

Toxoplasmosis. It's a cousin to coccidia and its life cycle is similar with one large exception: Coccidia doesn't constitute a public heath problem; toxoplasmosis does. This particular protozoan doesn't just cause pneumonia, high fevers, and intestinal problems in cats — it's also transmittable from one species to another. It can cause systemic diseases and miscarriages in pregnant women and can affect a human fetus.

Cats acquire toxoplasmosis from eating prey that has it or raw meat containing it. People acquire the disease from a cat by not cleaning out litter boxes daily, or by allowing the animal to play in a child's sandbox, or the garden, or to go out hunting. Don't panic. A routine stool analysis can detect toxoplasmosis in your cat, and prescribed medication can cure it. Better, though, to prevent it by controlling your cat's play areas and cleaning out the litter box daily. If you're pregnant, definitely have someone else clean out the litter box.

FELINE ASTHMA

As with people, an asthma attack in a cat can become an emergency situation is a very short time. If the attack is acute, you can't miss it. The animal is gasping, mouth agape, tongue hanging out, and coughing. If the attack is mild, there will be panting, heavy breathing, lethargy, and the animal will not be himself. If the attack is very mild, some difficulty in breathing being the only evidence, you may not notice a change of behavior or condition for two or three days.

Initially, we'll assume the attack, regardless of the degree of intensity, is your first experience with feline asthma. What can you do?

If you have an over-the-counter antihistamine on hand, such as a cold tablet, administer a children's size dose (see page 116 for dosage). *Make sure the antihistamine doesn't contain aspirin, which is toxic to cats.* Place the cat in a cool room and turn up the air conditioner. The cool air constricts blood vessels in the bronchial tubes and allows the animal to breathe a little easier. Now call a veterinarian or an emergency veterinary clinic. If possible, have someone do that while you're giving the cat a pill. Your cat may need professional help soon.

Now let's suppose you've been through it all before. Your cat has a history of feline asthma, you've been to a veterinarian, and have been administering the control medication prescribed. Prepare yourself. Ask your veterinarian about increasing dosage in case of an attack, and don't allow your supply of medication to run low. If you reach for it, and it's not there, and your veterinarian is out of town, you *must* go to an emergency clinic immediately.

THE CARDIOVASCULAR SYSTEM

The most important life support system in any living organism, the cardiovascular network, centers on the heart and includes all the blood vessels leading to and from it. The system's job is to supply nutrients, carried by the blood, to all parts of the body and to remove waste materials from those parts. That's pretty simplistic, but essentially that's the way the system works. Anything causing a disfunction or interruption of the process is going to produce problems. First aid for those problems primarily comes down to recognizing that the animal has a problem and seeking veterinary help. There is little else you can do.

Obvious Signs. A sudden collapse or fainting is an obvious indication of trouble, but it doesn't mean the heart has stopped, only that it is unable to function normally.

Milder Signs of a problem include difficulty in breathing or loss of breath, listlessness, and progressive weakness. There may also be a loss of appetite — the animal is so busy trying to keep its circulation going that it doesn't want to eat. Other mild signs are pale inner mouth membranes and cold paws and pads.

Advanced Signs. Eventually, a dropsylike swelling of the extremities due to the accumulation of water, possible abdominal swelling, lameness in the hindquarters which can progress to paralysis, and a drop in normal body temperature (normal for a cat is 101 to 102 degrees F.).

Treatment. Unfortunately, first aid in the generally accepted sense of the term is very limited. However, in the event of an acute, emergency situation: keep the cat as quiet, comfortable, and calm as possible; keep human handling to a minimum; and do not attempt to administer any oral medication. The very act of getting the medicine into the animal will only place greater stress on an already weakened system. Get your cat to a veterinarian.

Congenital Cardiovascular Problems. These show up early on in life, generally after weaning, when the kitten should become more active. Kittens that play a little, then quit, may have such problems. So may kittens who remain stunted in growth, or who faint or pass out on occasion. Common causes for this may be heart valve or septal defects, similar to the "blue baby" condition in humans and directly related to the improper formation of the heart during pregnancy. The prognosis for young cats so affected — and there's no gentler way of stating it — is grave.

Acquired Cardiovascular Problems. Though they used to be thought of as rare in animals — either they were born with them or didn't have them — the fact that these problems do exist has become increasingly accepted as a result of greatly improved diagnostic techniques. In the future, the occurrence of acquired problems will probably increase simply because they are now being correctly diagnosed.

Most Common Cause of Cardiovascular Trouble. It's the old enemy: infection. A bad tooth, an infected middle or inner ear, or an abscess, for example. Bacteria from any one of them can stage a mass invasion of the bloodstream. A system fighting infection isn't up to coping with such sudden, intensive abuse, the bacteria affect the heart muscle and inflame it, and the heart cannot function as it should. The walls of a heart so affected may become weakened or thin, and the heart itself may become enlarged. This condition is medically referred to as *cardiomyopathy*. An enlarged heart can't do its job pumping blood and the red corpuscles get into a gridlock situation, making it impossible for them to perform their nutrient-delivering and cleansing task. The result is congestive heart failure.

We suggest you now reread the preceding paragraphs, further familiarize yourself with signs of cardiovascular distress, and be alert for them, particlularly if your cat has frequent infections.

To conclude, your best defense against cardiovascular disease is to maintain a healthy cat. Have it neutered, try to keep it out of fights, and maintain a regular checkup schedule.

THE URINARY SYSTEM

Urinary problems can result from a number of causes and can involve any part of the urinary tract: kidneys, ureter, bladder, and urethra. Signs to look for include bloody urine, depression, loss of appetite, cries of distress, constant licking in the urinary area, and a change in drinking habits. The source of the problem and its treatment are for a doctor to determine. Our intention here is to assist you in recognizing that a problem exists and to provide information on basic preventive measures.

You should know that kidney problems can be congenital and that cats born with them don't survive very long: They're sickly, drink a lot of water trying to dilute the toxins in their systems, and are most often incurable. Kidney problems as a result of severe trauma — a fall or an encounter with a car — are fairly common, but can be compensated for in an otherwise healthy cat to the point of full recovery.

Cats are notorious for their conservation of water. When all is well with their urinary system, they drink very little. *Any change* in your cat's drinking habits, especially an urge to drink more than usual, should be noted and called to your veterinarian's attention. Excessive thirst doesn't come naturally to felines and usually indicates there's something wrong in the urinary system.

Urinary Problems and Diet. Hundreds of pages of research have found that diet plays a very important part in kidney and bladder dysfunctions. The same research strongly concludes that an incorrect diet ultimately leads to FUS (feline urethral syndrome), which will be discussed as a separate subject in this section.

Cats produce sandlike crystals in their kidneys. It's a normal part of their metabolism, and, under normal conditions, these crystals pass from kidneys to bladder to be discharged through the urethra. However, diets high in ash content, especially magnesium, and diets low in animal protein tend to create conditions that produce more of these crystals than the animal can metabolize. A surplus of crystals may block up the kidneys, bladder, and urethra creating a toxic condition (uremia) that can become critical in a very short period of time. To prevent this, select a diet low in ash and magnesium and higher in animal protein. Provide plenty of fresh water and check with your veterinarian regarding both the diet and any supplements your cat may require.

Kidney Diseases. Cancer of the kidneys is fairly common in young kittens and is also found in older cats, but it is not the dominant cause of renal (kidney) failure. Nor are parasites. It's nephritis:

infections of the kidney caused by bacterial infections elsewhere on the body as an extension of the bacteria's dirty work. The results of nephritis are usually acute. The animal evidences a loss of appetite, runs a fever, and either increases or decreases its urinary activity. There is no first aid treatment; see your veterinarian soon.

Inflammation of the Bladder. The medical term is cystisis, and it is the most common urinary problem found in cats. Despite frequent occurrence, the causes are not always understood, but primary infection isn't one of them. Cats don't catch a cold in the bladder. A true bladder infection is usually related to some other problem, such as a kidney infection or an improper diet which intensifies the concentration of the urine and causes a buildup of those sandlike crystals.

A bladder infection can also be caused by a dirty litter pan, which some cats simply refuse to use because it's not cleaned. Since they've been trained not to urinate anywhere else, they hold their water. Up goes the pH of the urine, and the animal is subject to cystisis, unless it calls its owner's attention to the dirty litter pan by relieving itself elsewhere. The bathtub or shower stall are considered acceptable substitutes by a cat under such stress. Obviously, prevention in this case calls for keeping your cat's litter pan clean.

FUS (Feline Urethral Syndrome). Here, the urethra itself has become blocked by conglomerates of the crystals. The animal is unable to urinate, or at best can relieve itself of only a few drops at a time. The situation is very serious in any case, but more serious with male cats because their urethral opening is smaller than the female's.

A cat so affected will strain frequently, as though constipated. The bladder will continue to fill, and the distress mounts until the bladder becomes filled to the point where it creates enough pressure to cause kidney shutdown.

If you suspect your cat is experiencing such a problem, you can very, very gently palpate (squeeze) the bladder just in front of the hind legs to find out if it is overfull. Be extremely careful, because a distended bladder is easily ruptured. Your cat will let you know that he or she doesn't appreciate the palpating, but its displeasure will only confirm that an immediate trip to your veterinarian is necessary.

Urinary Incontinence. A condition opposite that of FUS, incontinence can be congenital in its origins or the result of a trauma in which the bladder was ruptured, bladder inflammation, feline leukemia, or lack of hormonal control in older, spayed females. The signs are always the same: The cat is urinating all over the place.

If the cause is congenital or the result of trauma, and damage is not too extensive, surgery may correct the condition. If caused by feline leukemia or bladder inflammation, prescribed medication can help. Or if lack of hormonal control is involved, a regimen of hormone therapy may have to be given. Don't try to figure out the cause of your cat's problem. Take your cat, and a urine sample, to your veterinarian.

THE REPRODUCTIVE SYSTEM

There is little to be said here from a first aid standpoint, but a great deal to be said about preventive medicine.

Ninety-nine percent of all reproductive system problems can be totally and *easily* avoided by having your cat neutered early in life. The only reason *not* to have your cat neutered is if he or she has value as a breeder. The most conservative estimate of the cat population in the United States is 240 million. Estimates are that only a third of that number are housed, and a female can produce four to six kittens every six months. Even if the number of males and females in this figure were equally divided and monogamous, the number of new kittens possible per year is staggering.

With males, we recommend neutering between seven to nine months at the latest. If he starts spraying, you've waited too long. So don't wait: Spare the animal the fighting, infections, and abscesses that are inevitable if you put things off.

Females should be spayed before the first heat, which usually occurs at five to six months of age. We stress *before*, since a female cat can become pregnant at that age, and she is in no way ready for it. Pregnancy will place a great strain on the system, often resulting in birth defects, and she may not be able to nurse, resulting in seriously malnourished kittens. This is why breeders use year-old, or older, queens. In addition, early spaying prevents later problems, including mammary tumors, uterine infections, and uterine tumors. If a female is allowed to go through a heat before spaying, those problems may still arise in later life, because estrogen is stored in the system as a result of the heat.

Detection of Heat. If you've never been through a cat's heat before, the experience can be quite distressing. There is much rolling on the floor, hindquarters are held high with her tail erect, appetite falls off, and house-training gets ignored. Some purebreds (Siamese, for instance), are very vocal about the event.

Rushing your cat to the veterinarian for spaying now isn't going to solve the problem overnight. Besides, most vets prefer not to spay during heat. The animal's blood vessels, being engorged, are more apt to bleed during spaying and increase the possibility of anemia after surgery. However, some females can stay in heat until after they are bred, in which case you may have no choice but to spay while the cat is still in heat.

Infections of the Reproductive Tract in Unspayed Females. These are very common, even among cats who haven't had a litter or two. When in heat, the system is very susceptible to infection because it's getting ready for kittens. It's warm, full of fluid, has an extra blood supply, and, as a result, is the perfect breeding place for bacteria.

The signs of such infections are obvious, or should be to even the most casual of owners/observers. The cat isn't eating as it has been and may be drinking more water, which is a certain indication, anytime, of trouble. The cat will be using the litter pan or going outside to relieve itself more often, but will be less active. If you're fortunate, the clearest sign will be a discharge from the vulva. If there is an infection and no discharge, however, there is in all probability some sort of blockage, and the animal's abdomen may become distended. The infection will spread, and the cat will become toxic and can die very quickly. See your veterinarian as soon as possible. The risk is greater, and so is the expense of surgery, but you now have no choice and *must* have your cat spayed if you want to try to save her.

Whelping. Whether by your choice or not, your cat is pregnant. Since we're dealing here with the great, average, American house cat and not a purebred who would likely be under a breeder's care, prepare a whelping area in which she can bring forth her young. Sixty-three days from conception (give or take three or four), that little kitten you found irresistible will become a mother, a Queen. If you're aware she's been bred, have her examined shortly after the act. If her pregnancy comes as a complete surprise, a visit to the veterinarian will be in order during the fourth or fifth week to determine whether or not any problems exist and to make sure the lady is receiving the proper diet.

It's best to control the animal's wanderings. This is no hard task if the mother-to-be is an indoor cat, but if she's the outdoor type, limit her roaming with a leash. She's vulnerable now and she's apt to decide on an outdoor spot in which to give birth that would endanger both her and her kittens.

How do you encourage your cat to use a whelping place? Two ways. If she's an indoor cat, it could be a box, a wicker basket, or a standard carrier furnished with a few of the animal's favorite things. It has to be a place in which the cat will feel secure and comfortable. In addition, it has to be at once private and accessible. The cat may not approve of your designated place, though, and may choose one of her own. Perhaps behind a chair, a sofa, or in a closet. Don't try to change her mind. Once it's made up there's little you can do about it, and you'll only get yourself, and her, upset by trying.

If your expectant mother is an outdoor cat, concentrate on encouraging her to stay indoors. Introduce her to a very private place of her own inside, complete with a litter pan filled with dirt. Although she may seem to accept her in-home location, don't be too sure and do be watchful, because there's no guarantee she has accepted it enough to give birth in it and could, if given the opportunity, slip away. If you fail completely, and your outdoor cat simply can't adjust to indoor living, about all you can do is try to establish a safe birthing place outside and hope she'll use it when the time comes. An enclosed porch, if you have one, may serve nicely as a compromise.

We have to assume now that you've been successful and that your cat is more or less under your supervision when the big day arrives. In most cases, she'd rather do it alone, so keep your distance but be ready to help if needed. We recommend against having young children present unless they don't insist on handling the newborns upon arrival.

As for your cat, as she prepares to give birth she will be down, straining in labor. It may take up to an hour before the first kitten is born. If it's more than an hour, call your veterinarian for a consultation. An hour between the delivery of each kitten is not unusual and, as deliveries go on, the time between them will increase. She'll be tired, her uterus will be tired, but that doesn't mean there are no more kittens to be born.

Normally, the queen will clean each kitten, breaking the umbilical cord in the process. If she doesn't, or if she is so domesticated she's lost some of her maternal instincts, you will have to do it for her. Take the kitten from her, break the placenta, clean the kitten's face with a warm, moist towel, and clean out its mouth with your fingers. Next, pinch off the cord with your fingertips about an inch from the body and apply a mild first aid cream to the break. Finally, hold the kitten, head down, in one hand and gently massage it with the other to encourage breathing before giving it back to its mother.

Once the litter is complete, remove the queen and her family from their maternity ward, replace the soiled bedding with clean bedding and put mother and kittens back in it. The youngsters should start nursing soon after whelping. If their mother allows them to stay near her and nurse away, fine. But if she doesn't, or if the kittens are nursing and vocally protesting because they're not getting enough milk, be prepared to take over. Have on hand a formula for orphan kittens. You can get it at any pet store and you can give it using a premie bottle or an eyedropper.

The next morning, take queen and kittens to your veterinarian. Antibiotics will be given to her to prevent infection along with a hormonal injection. Her family will be checked over to make sure all is in good order, and you will find out for certain whether there are any kittens yet to be born. Many kittens have first seen the light of day when their mother, brothers, and sisters have been brought in for their first, post-whelping checkup.

The next family checkup should take place when the kittens are four to five weeks old. Stool samples for mother and kittens will be needed to determine if parasites are present, and any shots required can either be given or scheduled for a later date.

Difficult Deliveries. Using a soft, wet, warm towel, grasp gently but firmly whatever part of the kitten is visible. As the mother contracts, you pull. Don't be weak about it. If that kitten doesn't come out in two or three minutes, you could lose the kitten being born and the kittens yet to be born. The technique described is particularly important in cases of breech births, where there is danger of the umbilical cord becoming pinched and the oxygen supply being cut off before the kitten starts breathing on its own.

NEUROLOGICAL PROBLEMS

Since exactly how the brain functions is often a mystery, and may remain one for years to come, the problems directly affecting the brain are, except for a major accident, the most upsetting to the cat owner. They're not easily comprehended, may have local or widespread symptoms, and usually happen suddenly. For the most part, there seems to be no cause and nothing to blame for the animal's condition.

We do know this: the brain is the mainframe computer of the body's central nervous system and works on a combination of electricity, hormones, and electrolytes (minerals). Any mixup in communication between the brain and other parts of the nervous system results in a multitude of signs that something is definitely wrong. These signs include staggering, walking in circles, seizures, head tilting to one side, paralysis of one hind leg, paralysis of the tail, or paralysis to the point where the animal is unable to walk at all.

Why do any or all of the above occur? An obvious cause would be an injury to the brain from a traumatic accident. A less obvious cause would be a secondary factor related to another problem existent in the animal's system.

Heredity is one such possibility, because some breeds are more susceptible to disorders of the central nervous system than others. Certain digestive problems that interfere with the proper utilization of food, and the resulting chemical imbalance of the system, are another possible cause. If the liver fails to detoxify the blood properly, the toxic blood will be pumped through the system by the heart and, eventually, affect brain function. Chronic diarrhea or constipation can, and does, short out the nervous system by interfering with electrolyte balance and the elimination of toxins. Many bacterial organisms and viral infections, including those that cause feline leukemia, peritonitis, and rabies can also affect the central nervous system. Feline distemper, for instance, which kittens can acquire from the mother, is the most common of all viral infections. Parasitic larval migration, heat stroke, dietary deficiencies, brain tumors, certain antibiotics, and insecticides can all cause neurological problems.

Vestibular Syndrome. This condition can be brought on by many things, including feline leukemia, but whatever brings it on usually does so very suddenly by attacking the auditory and vestibular nerve in the inner ear. If it's able to walk at all, the cat is staggering or moving in circles with its eyes jerking back and forth. The onset is very disturbing, but the prognosis is good if the animal is promptly treated by a veterinarian. In addition to being caused by viral infections, vestibular syndrome can result from trauma, certain antibiotics, or a tumor, in which case the onset will not be sudden. It can also be hereditary, particularly with the Siamese or Burmese, and will show itself early in life by inordinate head tilting and deafness.

Most neurological problems don't lend themselves to first aid. However, interpreting the signs properly may help during your call to a veterinarian if and when any problems arise. We'll list the probable, or related, causes of neurological problems first, then the signs that most often accompany them.

Hereditary, Infection, Dietary, Tumor. Abnormal behavior, most commonly depression, is symptomatic. The animal acts dumb, doesn't respond to sound or light, and shuns even its favorite toy. It may bump into the wall, then step back and wait for the wall to get out of the way before bumping into it again. Its gait will be irregular, with front feet goosestepping. It may wobble drunkenly or move only in circles. If the cat shakes its head, usually tilted to one side or the other, it may fall down. There's nothing subtle about these signs; you can't miss them.

Trauma, Heat Stroke, Circulatory. The cat is normal one minute, then experiences one or more of the above signs followed by loss of conciousness, loss of control over bodily functions, and partial or complete paralysis. If a trauma is the cause, the area or areas paralyzed depend on the location of the injury. A lower spinal injury would paralyze the hindquarters; a neck or high cervical (lower brain) injury would affect all four legs. We recommend that you keep these facts in mind when about to move an injured, partially paralyzed cat in order to prevent further damage to the trauma center. See the text on spine fractures (page 32) for specific methods of handling.

Although we have previously commented that there are no first aid measures available to the cat owner when neurological problems arise, there are a few things that can be applied in case of emergency. All such measures must be promptly followed by a trip to your veterinarian.

Loss of Consciousness. Try to determine your cat's level of consciousness. If semiconscious, the cat will be aware of what's going on and will most likely respond to you. If it doesn't, and all the signs of shock are present — shallow breathing, pale lip and mouth membranes, cool paws indicating a drop in body temperature — the animal is unconscious. Treat as you would for shock.

If a loss of consciousness is the result of head trauma, and the wound is superficial, apply slight pressure to control any hemorrhaging and a light bandage, but do not flush the wound. Flushing might force foreign material into the cranial cavity.

Seizures. If seizures are due to hereditary causes, they cannot always be treated. On the other hand, seizures caused by bacteria, viruses, and parasites can be avoided through regular checkups, proper vaccination, and proper diet or diet supplements. Most seizures are over very quickly, but if one lasts for five to ten minutes, poisoning of some kind may be the cause, and the cat should see a veterinarian immediately.

One of the problems with seizures in cats is that a cat doesn't show many signs that it's about to have one. It *may* go hide in a corner, become more vocal or restless, or evidence muscle spasms just before seizuring. If you're on the spot when a seizure occurs, use a mild restraint (Figure 52) to protect the animal from injuring itself further. Reduce all exterior stimuli by lowering the lights and household sounds.

After a short seizure, the animal will be disoriented. Do not feed it or give it a large quantity of water. Place it in a box or carrier and leave it alone. There's no immediate emergency unless a second seizure occurs soon after the first, but any seizure should be followed by a visit to your veterinarian.

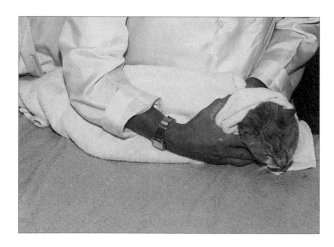

Figure 52. Place cat on a blanket or towel. Completely wrap body and legs, but leave head exposed so the animal can breathe.

If the seizure is severe, the cat will convulse, tremors will be apparent, and the animal will most likely fall unconscious. If it is unconscious, administer CPR. If it isn't, don't try it. Cats experiencing seizures are not aggressive, but they have no control over themselves. The restraint shown in Figure 52, therefore, serves the dual purpose of protecting both you and your pet.

AN OVERVIEW OF POISONS

Before we enter into specifics, we'd like to make a few pertinent suggestions concerning poisons in general.

✛ If you have poisons in or around the house, take the same precaution with a cat that you would with a child: keep any poisonous substances *well* out of reach.

✛ Keep the package insert listing the hazardous potential of the substance, because knowing the name of the poison taken is of significant help to a veterinarian when measures beyond the home-administered variety are necessary. Package inserts and labels also carry information on antidotes. Since the hazards of poisons are the same for cats as they are for people, the antidotes are the same.

✛ Prepare a poison first aid kit containing a stomach-coating agent, hydrogen peroxide, milk of magnesia, and activated charcoal. Contact your veterinarian for the phone number of the local poison control center. You may need it should a poisoning occur and you are unable to reach medical help. The chance of this happening is highly unlikely, what with veterinary emergency clinics and doctors on call, but be prepared for it just in case.

✛ If your cat comes in contact with a toxic substance, either remove the animal from the source or the source from the animal.

Basic Treatment for Ingested Poisons. Provided the substance is not acid, alkaline, or a petroleum product, and you actually saw it ingested, induce vomiting and save some of the vomitus for veterinary examination.

If the substance is acid, alkaline, or petroleum, dilute its toxicity by having the cat drink some milk, mineral oil, or vegetable oil. Administer in small portions — a teaspoon or tablespoon at a time — to avoid inhalation by the animal. Repeat this dosage every ten to fifteen minutes.

Neutralize swallowed acid by administering antacid in liquid form: 1 teaspoon or tablespoon at a time, given frequently.

Neutralize alkali, such as toilet bowl cleaner, by administering a 50 percent vinegar, 50 percent water solution in frequent dosages of 1 teaspoon or tablespoon at a time.

After treating for an acid, alkaline, or petroleum poisoning, and after all vomiting has ceased, force-feed the cat plain water to flush out its system. You should then prepare an emulsion of stomach-coating agent and activated charcoal that is about as thick as a milk shake. There is no set dosage. Use common sense depending on the size of the cat.

If the animal is depressed, administer a mild stimulant. One tablespoon of weak tea with sugar or the same amount of a room temperature carbonated cola given every half hour will provide all the stimulation required.

Some poisons cause seizures. If your cat is conscious, there's nothing you can do beyond wrapping it in a towel until the seizure passes or until you can get the animal to a veterinarian. If the cat is unconscious, transport it to the veterinarian in a box or carrier tilted so that the animal's head is lower than its body. Be prepared to administer CPR along the way should breathing become labored by getting someone else to drive, and to provide the doctor with the name of the substance ingested.

Next, we're going to mention several specific sources of toxic substances that cats would ordinarily have nothing to do with unless the cat were a curious kitten. First, though, take a look at a basic first aid measure (Figures 53A-53C) you'll have to use to induce vomiting if your cat ever samples or is given something that is poisonous and will make it very sick.

HOUSEHOLD POISONS

Analgesics. One extra-strength headache tablet or caplet containing aspirin or acetaminophen can kill a cat. Shocking, but very true. Cats can't metabolize those chemicals. One dose will last up to forty-eight hours in the body. If another dose is administered too

Figures 53A, 53B, 53C. Full body and head restraint is required. Force open mouth by placing one hand on the cat's head and using your thumb to apply pressure to the corner of its jaw (A). Insert index finger of free hand down throat to induce vomiting (B), or, using a paper cup, pour a small amount of peroxide (C) down throat instead.

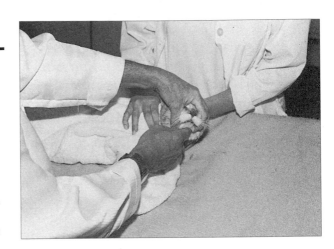

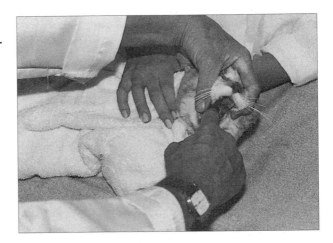

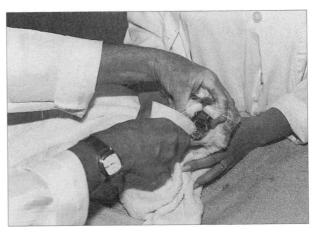

soon thereafter, the toxic buildup can reach lethal levels. Never give a headache pill to your cat unless you have been advised that it's safe to do so by your veterinarian.

Early signs that a cat has gotten into the medicine cabinet and has had one pill too many include vomiting, depression, and loss of appetite. Subsequent signs are hyperventilation, nervousness, muscular weakness, and tremors. If vomiting continues, it may eventually contain blood. If you're aware of the cat's dangerous ingestion, induce vomiting with a solution of salt and water or plain hydrogen peroxide (Figure 53C) and see your veterinarian.

Caffeine and Chocolate. Very few cats we know have ever taken a sip of coffee or tea, or a bite of chocolate, but if yours decides either is to its liking — and you see it indulge itself — induce vomiting with the salt-water solution or hydrogen peroxide and get medical help. Early signs of ingestion include restlessness and may eventually lead to staggering, tremors, coma, and death.

Antifreeze and Deicer Fluid. Cats love them because they apparently have a sweet taste. Unless you see it happen, you'll have no idea what's wrong with the animal.

It takes veterinary tests to determine that your cat is drunk and subject to severe kidney damage as a result of its tippling. Interestingly enough, the antidote for such feline imbibing is 100 proof vodka, given intravenously. If you see your cat lapping up an antifreeze or deicer spill, induce vomiting immediately and see your veterinarian.

Mild Detergents. Cat's won't eat them, but, if you spill some, a cat will lick its paws after stepping in the spill. Dishwasher and other laundry detergents aren't usually serious. They may produce some burning of the skin or mouth, but if enough is swallowed, vomiting and diarrhea will ensue. If you see it happen, flush the affected skin areas and the mouth with water. You may then give the cat milk to drink, followed by a stomach-coating agent which you administer with an eyedropper, as was shown in Figure 35A on page 64.

Strong Detergents. These include toilet bowl and glass cleaners.

Being more caustic than mild detergents, they cause greater damage to the skin and mouth and can cause ulceration of the esophagus and stomach. If you're on the scene, *do not induce vomiting.* Flush the exterior where there was contact, then give milk and administer a stomach-coating agent before contacting your veterinarian.

Shampoos. The medicated variety, particularly those intended to control dandruff, can be quite toxic to cats. Acute vomiting and diarrhea follow ingestion and are, in turn, followed by damage to the central nervous system and kidneys. Administer a stomach-coating agent and see your veterinarian immediately.

Drain Cleaners. Extremely caustic, these harsh chemicals result in serious external and internal damage. If external, secure the help of another person and hold the animal under a cold water faucet while the affected area is flushed, flushed, and flushed some more. Then neutralize what cleaner remains on the skin with milk or vinegar. If internal, there is the strong possibility of severe damage to the esophagus and stomach. Do not induce vomiting, since it will only recycle the chemical. Immediate medical attention is required.

Lead. Even today, in spite of all the legislation against using lead-based paint for home and business interiors, lead poisoning is fairly common in pets. A can of old paint gets spilled, walked in, and licked off. An equally old, leaky dry cell battery or a fishing sinker gets teethed on by a kitten. A bird downed by lead shot is eaten by a cat out hunting for a snack. There are no acute signs of lead poisoning. It's insidious, persistent, and manifests itself quite slowly. The gradual signs of lead poisoning include vomiting, diarrhea, muscle weakness, and loss of energy. Eventually, these will be followed by anemia and disorders of the central nervous system.

The first aid measures are purely preventive. Make certain the cat's habitat is free of lead-bearing compounds, and, if you witness the animal ingesting anything you even suspect contains lead, see your veterinarian right away.

Lawn Products. Once on the lawn, it's usually not a toxic problem, but fertilizer has been mistaken for kitty litter by a house-trained cat caught short. If yours happens to make the same mistake, vomiting and diarrhea will follow. You may administer a stomach-coating agent to settle things down, but if the distress continues for anything over twenty-four hours consult your veterinarian.

Weed killers and insecticides, more often than not, contain an organic phosphate. In general, these are extremely toxic to cats. Ingestion will produce vomiting, diarrhea, difficulty in breathing, muscle weakness, and, over a period of time, liver damage. If you're aware such a chemical has been swallowed, encourage vomiting, flush the paws and mouth with water, and see your veterinarian. And if you have insecticides containing chlorinated hydrocarbons, get rid of them. Once swallowed by your cat, there's no treatment and no antidote — only death.

Fuels and Solvents. These include any petroleum product as well as turpentine. Whether walked through and licked off or absorbed through the skin, they are all toxic to cats. If left untreated, they can be fatally toxic. When enough of these materials are absorbed, or their fumes inhaled, further breathing will become difficult. There will be vomiting, diarrhea, and eventual failure of the kidneys, liver, and central nervous system. First aid calls for the area affected to be flushed thoroughly with cool water, then generously rubbed with mineral oil. You may then wash off the mineral oil with a mild soap or shampoo. *Do not try to cause or encourage vomiting.*

Paint. If it's an oil-based paint or stain, treat as a solvent. If it's water-based, simply wash it off. For your cat's sake, *don't ever use turpentine to remove paint from your cat.*

Rodenticides. Pellets containing strychnine are outlawed in most states, but some pellets intended for moles may still be around. Your cat wouldn't eat the pellets, but it might catch and eat the poisoned mole. In which case, the signs will be dramatic. The animal will become very hyperactive, experience severe muscle tremors, and overact to light, sound, and touch. If you know these actions have been caused by strychnine, induce vomiting and see your veterinarian. If you're not sure strychnine is the cause and your cat's behaving as just described, don't do anything except see your veterinarian. Fast. In the past, rodenticides containing coumarins were not considered dangerous, and they weren't. Nowadays however, products containing coumarin have been enhanced with a second-stage product. This product doesn't break down in a cat's system the way plain coumarin did. A cat won't eat the rodenticide containing "new improved" coumarin, but it may devour the rodent that has eaten it. This new coumarin lingers in the system and has a residual effect that can be fatal to a cat.

If you see your cat making a meal of a mouse that you suspect might contain coumarin, induce vomiting and arrange to see your veterinarian. If you don't see it happen, certain signs will alert you to the fact that it has. The most obvious of these are black and blue nails, diarrhea or vomit containing blood, or all of the above. Veterinary treatment is required.

Household Insecticides. Read the product label. If it cautions against residual side effects in animals and humans, don't use it. If you do, and use it too often, you'll be creating a situation similar to the one just discussed regarding coumarin.

Animal Insecticides. Again, read the label. The only two insecticides that can safely be used on a cat are the pure pyrethrins and rotenone, and only if they contain no enhancers that can produce a residual effect. Stay away from the long-term stuff used to combat fleas and other pests in any form — spray, powder, dip, or collar — they usually contain organic phosphates which your cat may not be able to tolerate and which can cause vomiting, diarrhea, muscular weakness, and/or persistent skin problems.

Stay away from insecticides that are safe for older cats if you have a younger cat and vice versa. Stay away from *all* shampoos that aren't clearly marked as being harmless to cats, and once you have your hands on one that is safe, use it often. It will do just as good a job of keeping your cat free of creepy-crawly things as a spray or powder, while lowering your risk of creating a bigger problem.

Disposable, Ready-Made Enema Solutions. These over-the-counter potions in little plastic squeeze bottles are highly effective with humans, but are toxic if ingested by an older or debilitated cat, since they contain sodium phosphate. If retained and absorbed by the animal's system, sodium phosphate will cause severe depression, weakness, convulsions, and death. If you have any of these solutions in your house, make sure they're cat-proofed.

POISONOUS PLANTS

What is presented here is by no means a total list. It would require an entire book to cover all geographic areas and all the plants in each which can be toxic to cats, so we selected the most commonly found backyard varieties and houseplants. If you have any of the plants listed below in or around your home, find a way to keep your cat away from them, even if it means fencing them in (the plants, not the cat). Unless you see your cat eat one of them, you won't know that a plant is causing the animal's problem. It's unlikely an older cat will have anything to do with plants. Kittens, far more curious and adventuresome than their elders, must be watched more carefully.

An older cat might graze on some grass and experience a little vomiting nor diarrhea because of it, but such occurrences are neither serious nor frequent. Cats are carnivores, remember. Eating vegetables doesn't and shouldn't come naturally to them, but if you give your cat leftover vegetables with its food you can inadvertently train it to be more tolerant of flora. Another thing we advise against is letting your cat to use a planter or flower pot as a litter box.

The Least Irritating. Elephant-ear, philodendron, Jack-in-the-pulpit, and skunk-cabbage are irritating, cause a lot of drooling, and some swelling of membranes. To treat their effects, flush the mouth with water.

The Mildly Irritating. Amaryllis, daffodils, wisteria, and mushrooms cause stomach irritation and vomiting. The treatment is to restrict food and water, and to administer a stomach-coating agent.

Irritating. English ivy, iris, pokeweed, Japanese yew, clematis, and bird-of-paradise all cause intestinal cramps, vomiting and diarrhea. Administer a stomach-coating agent.

Severly Irritating. Christmas-candle, box bush, English holly, honeysuckle, poinsettia, and privet hedge cause intestinal cramps, vomiting, diarrhea, and central nervous system disorders. Your cat will be obviously get sick after ingesting any one of them. Administer a stomach-coating agent and call your veterinarian.

Toxic. Foxglove, lily-of-the-valley, oleander, larkspur, hemlock, and taxus yew cause vomiting and abdominal pains, and can cause cardiac arrest. Administer a stomach-coating agent and transport the animal to a veterinarian.

Very Toxic. Apricot, cherry, and peach carry the danger of cyanide poisoning. The animal will experience extreme difficulty in breathing. See your veterinarian immediately.

Hallucinogens. Cats are very sensitive to marijuana. If ingested or even inhaled, their reaction is hyperactive in the extreme and often leads to death.

Nettles, Thistles, and Cactus. All can create a foreign body reaction. If ingested, intestinal complications will result. Administer emollients to soothe the bowel and encourage evacuation. Time is the cure.

✚ —— DRUG DOSAGES —— ✚

Please bear in mind that the following are suggested drug doses and those generally used. However, due to variations in animal size and health conditions, specific dose recommendations cannot be made. When in doubt, use a much lesser dose or consult a veterinarian.

NAME	DESCRIPTION	DOSAGE
Activated charcoal	*Universal antipoison, also reduces flatulence. Powder form must be mixed with water to the consistency of a milk shake.*	*1 teaspoon per pound, orally.*
Aloe vera cream	*Soothes burns and other skin irritations.*	*Apply liberally to area of skin 3 to 4 times daily.*
Ascorbic acid, Vitamin C	*Urinary acidifier; useful in cats with chronic cystitis.*	*100 mg tablet twice daily.*
Aspirin	*Lessens pain, reduces fever. Can be toxic to cats. Check with your veterinarian if possible.*	*1 children's aspirin (for adult cats only), no more often than every 2 or 3 days.*
Chlor-trimeton	*Antihistamine, decongestant.*	*1 to 2 times daily.*
Cough medicines	*Do not use on cats without veterinary advice, may cause adverse reactions.*	
DiGel	*Antacid, antigas remedy.*	*1 teaspoon as needed every ½ to 1 hour.*
Hydrogen peroxide	*Medicinal.*	*Wounds: apply full strength, then flush with water. To induce vomiting: 1 to 2 teaspoons orally every few minutes until vomiting occurs.*

Kaopectate	*Soothes irritated stomach and intestines. Used to treat vomiting and diarrhea, as well as certain poisonings.*	*Administer freely 1 to 2 teaspoons every 1 to 2 hours. If problem continues, check with your veterinarian.*
Metamucil	*For chronic constipation; stool softener.*	*1 teaspoon in food once or twice daily.*
Milk of magnesia	*Antacid, antidote. Used for vomiting; is an antitoxin.*	*1 teaspoon once or twice daily. For constipation: 1 to 3 teaspoons as needed.*
Mineral oil	*Laxative. Used externally to soften paint, absorb solvents such as gasoline, turpentine, and oil products.*	*1 to 2 teaspoons orally, can be mixed in canned food. External: Apply to hair coat, then wash with mild detergent.*
Pepto-Bismol	*Antacid, effective for vomiting and diarrhea.*	*1 to 2 teaspoons as needed; can be given frequently.*
Sodium bicarbonate	*Antacid; simple upset stomach remedy; antitoxin.*	*Orally: 1 teaspoon per 8 ounces of water. Administer 1 to 4 teaspoons of this solution as needed for upset stomach. Topically: for acid burns on skin, flush area thoroughly.*
Vinegar (acetic acid)	*Antialkaline, used to neutralize alkalis such as lye and common detergent.*	*Orally: 1 teaspoon per 8 ounces of water. Can administer freely. Skin: use against alkaline burns by flushing area freely.*

A

Abdomen, internal bleeding, 43
Abrasion, minor, 41
Abscess, 49, 75-76, 77
Abyssinian, breed-specific hereditary defects, 11
Acetic acid, 117
Acne, 75
Acquiring a cat, 3-4
    adult vs. kitten, 7
    checkup, 4
    indoor vs. outdoor, 8-9
    neutering, 9
    pet shops, 4
    purebred, 9-10
    refund or exchange, 4
    shelters, 4
    short hair vs. long hair, 7-8
    stray, 9
Activated charcoal, 116
Adoption fee, 4
Aloe vera cream, 116
Amaryllis (plant poisonous to cat), 114
Anal atresia, 6
Analgesic, 108, 110
Angora, breed-specific hereditary defects, 11
Animal bites to cat from cat, 47, 48, 49
    from dog, 49-50
    from snake, 50-51
Antifreeze, 110
Apricot (plant poisonous to cat), 115
Ascorbic acid, 116
Aspirin, 116
Asthma, 94

B

Bandaging techniques, 34-39
Bird-of-paradise (plant poisonous to cat), 115

Birth defects. See Congenital disorders and specific disorders
Blackheads, 75
Bladder infection, 13
    inflammation, 98
Blue-eyed gene, 11
Body mite, 79
Bone disorder, 10
Box bush (plant poisonous to cat), 115
Brain injury. See Neurological problems
Brain tumors, 6
Breech births, 103
Breeding, 9
Bruise, internal bleeding, 43
Brushing teeth, 85
Burns, 61, 62
    chemical, 64-66, 67, 68, 69
    electric, 69-70
    eye, 65, 67
    feet, 68, 69
    first-degree, 61, 62-63
    heat, 62-64
    from petroleum products, 67-68
    second-degree, 62
    third-degree, 62, 63-64
    from turpentine, 67-68

C

Cactus, 115
Caffeine, 110
Cardiomyopathy, 96
Cardiovascular system, 94-96
    acquired problems, 96
    congenital problems, 95-96
Cars. See also Traveling with a cat and cats, 25
Cartilage disorder, 10
Cat acquiring. See Acquiring a cat
    domesticity, 3
    history of, 3
    washing, 78

Cat bites, 47, *48,* 49
Cat food, 13. *See also* Diet
Cats, and cars, 25
Cerebellar hypoplasia, 6
Chemical burns, 64-*66, 67,* 68, *69*
Cherry (plant poisonous to cat), 115
Chest
    injury from fall, 47
    internal bleeding, 43
    wound, 39, *45*
Chin injury, 46
Chlor-trimeton, 116
Chocolate, 110
Choking, 88-*89*
Christmas-candle (plant poisonous
    to cat), 115
Claw. *See* Nails
Cleft palate, 5
Clematis (plant poisonous to cat),
    115
Coccidia, 93
Colitis, 7
Congenital disorders, 4-7. *See also
    specific disorder*
    cardiovascular, 95-96
    delayed disorders, 6
Convergent strabissness, 10
Cough medicine, 116
Coumarin, 112
CPR, *26,* 45
    and poison, 108
    and seizures, 106
    with spinal fracture, 34
Cross-eyedness, 10
Cryptorchidism, 6
Cutareba fly, 80
Cyanide, 115
Cystisis, 98

D

Daffodil (plant poisonous to cat),
    114

Deafness, 6, 11
Deicer fluid, 110
Detergent (as poison), 110-11
Diaphragmatic hernia, 5-6
Diarrhea, 90
Diet, 14-15
    for disorders, 15
    for newborn, 14
    for pregnant cat, 14
    and skin, 74
    traveling with a cat, 13
    and urinary problems, 97
DiGel, 116
Distemper, 4
Dog bites, 49-50
Drain cleaner (as poison), 111
Drug dosages, 116-17

E

Ear hematoma, 59
    inflammation, 57
    puncture wound, 56, *57,* 58
    torn or bitten, 59
Electrolytes, 27
Electric burns, 69-70
Elephant-ear (plant poisonous to
    cat), 114
Elizabethan collar, 75
Enema solution (as poison), 113
English holly (plant poisonous to
    cat), 115
English ivy (plant poisonous to cat),
    115
Evisceration, 43, *44*
Eye
    chemical burn, *65,* 67
    injury, 41, *42,* 43
    puncture wound, 53, *54,* 56

F

Fall injuries, 46-47

Federal veterinarian certificate, traveling with cat, 12
Feet, burns, 68, *69*
Feline asthma. *See* Asthma
Feline leukemia. *See* Leukemia
Feline urethral syndrome (FUS), 97, 98-99
First aid kit, traveling with cat, 12
Fish hook, 56, 87-88
Flea, 77-79
    shampooing for, 77
    spray, 77
    and tapeworm, 77, 92-93
Foxglove (plant poisonous to cat), 115
Fracture
    compound, 31
    jaw, 31-*32*
    leg, 27, *28, 29, 30*
    with open wound, 31
    ribs, 32, *35*
    simple, 27, *28, 29, 30*
    skull, 40
    spine, 32-*33,* 34, *34*
    tail, 31
Frostbite, 68-69
Fuels (as poison), 111
FUS. *See* Feline urethral syndrome (FUS)

G

Gatorade, 27
Gingivitis, 85-86

H

Hallucinogens, 115
Harness, traveling with cat, 12
Head injury, *38, 60*
Head mite, 79
Health certificate, traveling with cat, 12

Heat (female reproduction cycle), 100
Heimlich technique, 88-*89*
Hematoma, 59
Hemlock (plant poisonous to cat), 115
Hemorrhage, 37-40
Hereditary disease, 10-11
Hernia, 5-6
Hiding in car, 25
Honeysuckle (plant poisonous to cat), 115
Hookworm, 91-92
Hormone therapy, 99
Hydroencephalus, 5
Hydrogen peroxide, 116

I

Insecticides (as poison), 113
Internal bleeding
    abdomen, 43
    bruise, 43
    chest, 43
Internal injury, 43, 50
Internal parasites, 90-94
Iris (plant poisonous to cat), 115
Isometric exercise, 13, 14

J

Jack-in-the-pulpit (plant poisonous to cat), 114
Japanese yew (plant poisonous to cat), 115
Jaw
    fracture, 31-*32*
    injury from fall, 46-47

K

Kaopectate, 117
Kidney disease, 97-98

L

Laceration, large
  heavy bleeding, 37, *38, 39, 40*
  little bleeding, 34-35, *36,* 37
Larkspur (plant poisonous to cat), 115
Lawn products (as poison), 111
Lead (as poison), 111
Leash, traveling with cat, 13
Leg
  bandaging, *39*
  fracture, 27, *28, 29, 30*
Leukemia, 4, 104
Lice, 79
Lily-of-the-valley (plant poisonous to cat), 115
Litter
  and internal parasites, 90-94
  traveling with cat, 13
Liver disease, 6
Lyme disease, 80

M

Maggot, 81-82
Male spraying, 9
Mange mite, 79
Marijuana, 115
Metabolism disorder, 11
Metamucil, 117
Miliary dermatitis, 74
Milk of magnesia, 117
Mineral oil, 117
Mite, 79
Mouth, bleeding, 40
Mouth wash, *86*
Moving an injured cat, *19,* 20-25
  cardboard box, 19
  conscious cat, 20-*21, 22*
  unconscious cat, 20
Mushroom (plant poisonous to cat), 114
Muzzle, 23

N

Nails
  broken, 83-*84*
  clipping, *74,* 75, *83*
  ingrown, 82-83
Nephritis, 97-98
Nettle, 115
Neurological problems, 103-7
  causes, 105-6
  symptoms, 105-6
Neutering, 9, 100-101
Nose
  bleeding, 40, 59, 61
  cut, 59
  injury caused by foreign body, 61
Nursing, 102

O

Oleander (plant poisonous to cat), 115
Oral problems, 84-89. *See also specific types*
  foreign bodies, 86-*87, 88, 89*

P

Paint (as poison), 111
Parasites
  internal, 90-94
  skin, 77-82
Patent ductus arteriosis, 10
Patent fontanal, 5
Peach (plant poisonous to cat), 115
Pepto-Bismol, 117
Periodontitis, 86
Persian, breed-specific hereditary defects, 11
Philodendron (plant poisonous to cat), 114
Plants, poisonous, 114-15
Poinsettia (plant poisonous to cat), 115

Poison, 107-15
  household, 108-14
  plants, 114-15
  treatment, 107-8, *109*
Pokeweed (plant poisonous to cat),
  115
Polydactylism, 5
Porcupine quills, *55*-56
Pregnancy
  diet, 14
  and vaccination, 5
Preventive medicine, 73-117
Privet hedge (plant poisonous to
  cat), 115
Puncture wound
  to ear, 56, *57*, 58
  to eye, 53, *54*, 56
  gun shot, 58-59
  to skin, *52*, 53, 54-*55*, 56
Purebred cats, 9-10
  breed-specific hereditary de-
    fects, 10-11
Pustules, 75

Q

Quarantine, traveling with cat, 12

R

Reproductive system, 99-103
  female infections, 100-101
Restraining cast, *29*
Restraining an injured cat, 21, 22,
  23, 24, 25
Ribs, fracture, 32, *35*
Ringworm, 75
Rodenticide (as poison), 111-12
Roundworm, 90-91

S

Seizures, *106*-7
Shampoo (as poison), 111
Shock, 26-27

and CPR, *26*, 27
  definition, 26
  and snake bites, 50
  treating, 27
Siamese, breed-specific hereditary
  defects, 10
Skin and diet, 74
  general problems, 74-82
  loss of, 41
  puncture wound, *52*, 53, 54-*55*,
    56
Skull, fracture, 40
Skunk-cabbage (plant poisonous to
  cat), 114
Snake bites, 50-*51*
Sodium bicarbonate, 117
Solvents (as poison), 111
Spine, fracture, 32-*33*, 34, *34*
Stool, and internal parasites, 90-94
Stray cats, 9
Strychnine, 111

T

Tail, fracture, 31
Tapeworm, 92-93
  and fleas, 77, 92-93
Tartar, 84-85
Taxus yew (plant poisonous to cat),
  115
Temperature, 27
Thalidomide-type kitten, 5
Thistle, 115
Throat, choking, 88-*89*
Tick, 79
  and Lyme disease, 80
  removing, *80*
Tissue, loss of, 41
Toothbrush, *85*
Toothpaste, *85*
Toxoplasmosis, 93-94
Trauma, 19-70. *See also specific
  types*
  definition, 19

Traveling with a cat, 1_ _
    cats who cannot travel, _ 14
    commercial carrier, 12
    federal veterinarian certifi-
        cate, 12
    feeding enroute, 13
    first aid kit, 12
    harness, 12
    health certificate, 12
    leash, 13
    litter, 13
    pretrip considerations, 11-12
    quarantine, 12
    vaccination, 12

U

Umbilical hernia, 5
Uremia, 97
Urinary incontinence, 99
Urinary system, 96-99

V

Vaccination, 4, 5
    traveling with cat, 12
Vestibular syndrome, 104
Vinegar, 117
Viral infection, 4
Vitamin C, 116
Vomiting, 89
    and poison, 107-15

W

Warble, 80-*81*
Whelping, 101-3
Whipworm, 92
Wisteria (plant poisonous to cat), 114